Radicalization

Radicalization

Why Some People Choose the Path of Violence

Farhad Khosrokhavar

Translated by Jane Marie Todd

THE NEW PRESS
25 YEARS

NEW YORK
LONDON

The New Press gratefully acknowledges the Florence Gould Foundation for supporting the publication of this book.

© 2015 by Éditions de la Maison des sciences de l'homme
Translation © 2017 by The New Press

Requests for permission to reproduce selections from this book should be
mailed to: Permissions Department, The New Press, 120 Wall Street,
31st floor, New York, NY 10005.

Originally published in France as *Radicalisation* in 2015 by Éditions de la
Maison des sciences de l'homme, Paris
Published in the United States by The New Press, New York, 2017
Distributed by Perseus Distribution

ISBN 978-1-62097-268-7 (hc)
ISBN 978-1-62097-269-4 (e-book)
CIP data is available

The New Press publishes books that promote and enrich public discussion and understanding of the issues vital to our democracy and to a more equitable world. These
books are made possible by the enthusiasm of our readers; the support of a committed
group of donors, large and small; the collaboration of our many partners in the independent media and the not-for-profit sector; booksellers, who often hand-sell New
Press books; librarians; and above all by our authors.

www.thenewpress.com

Composition by Westchester Book Composition
This book was set in Electra

Printed in the United States of America

2 4 6 8 10 9 7 5 3 1

Contents

Introduction

The Notion of Radicalization

Before the attacks of September 11, 2001, radicalization was a marginal notion, both in the social sciences and in works attempting to make sense of political, religious, or social extremism. In the West, the literature devoted to "terrorist" movements[1] since the early nineteenth century was more intent on discussing their forms of action—acts of terrorism for some, resistance against the oppressor, the occupier, or the enemy for others—than on studying the processes leading up to the recourse to violence. Since the September 11 attacks, the United States has attempted to promote research on terrorism and the factors that might encourage it, and radicalization has become a key notion for explaining the genesis of groups that embrace violent action.

The term *radicalization* refers to the process by which an individual or group adopts a violent form of action directly linked to an extremist ideology with a political, social, or religious content that contests the established order at a political, social, or cultural level (Borum 2011; Wilner and Dubouloz 2010). The elaboration of the practical implications of that notion is, in current practice, undeniably linked to national security concerns and seeks to answer such questions as: How can we protect cities, individuals, and countries (especially those in the West but also, by extension, others) from attack?[2] How can we suppress extremists, especially radical Islamists, in order to reduce (to nothing, if possible) their destructive capacity? How can we fight against terrorist networks both within national borders and internationally? And, since these networks are often transnational, how can we establish connections and cooperate with other countries to put an end to their activities in several places at once? And how can we identify these networks and their leaders so as to be able to neutralize them?

What processes lead individuals to join extremist groups? How can we fight against the appeal of radical ideologies (jihadist Islam in the first place but also violent far-right and far-left views) in societies and, in particular, how do we fight "homegrown terrorism," centered not in a foreign country (the Middle East) but in Europe or, less commonly, in the United States, Australia, or Canada?

Another series of questions concerns the profile of those who embark on the path of radicalization: What are the typical profiles of people who become involved in terrorism in its new forms? How do groups constitute themselves, join together, and set in motion a violent action? How do they recruit their members? Who are their sympathizers? And by what criteria do these sympathizers embrace their radical vision, to the point of becoming directly involved in attacks? In short, how do passive sympathizers turn into active terrorists? Finally, how do we "deradicalize" those who have yielded to the attraction of extremists? In Great Britain, the United States, Norway, and Muslim countries (Saudi Arabia, Algeria, and others), procedures for deradicalization have been devised that combine group therapy, indoctrination sessions by "competent authorities" (imams for the radical Islamists), and follow-ups by the police and psychologists to direct the former radicals toward nonviolent behaviors.

Governments have called on the academic world, especially in the United States—but also, to a lesser degree, in Europe and in the often authoritarian regimes of the Middle East and elsewhere—to establish profiles of those with a potential for violent action based on a radical ideology, primarily jihadist Islam. Billions of dollars have been invested, either directly (by the U.S. intelligence services, especially Homeland Security, but also autonomously by cities, such as New York) or indirectly (through research grants), to remedy the lack of information on the subject. Radicalization, once a marginal theme, has become a major one, promoted by the Western nations and, at their impetus, by Muslim states or those affected by them (Singapore, Russia, China, and others), to gather the information necessary to thwart the mass violence perpetrated by small groups.

We have come to speak of a new form of low-intensity war, whose proliferation after the demise of the bipolar world (divided between two major powers, the United States and the Soviet Union), symbolized by the fall of the Berlin Wall in 1989, marked a major shift in the configuration of conflicts. That type of war, waged by guerrillas and by terrorist groups operating in cities who detonate explosive charges in suicide attacks, cannot be combated effectively by traditional armies without profound modifications in their way of doing battle and collecting information.

Since the 1990s, the West has witnessed the appearance of homegrown terrorists, radical Islamists born and raised in Europe or the United States. For example, Khaled Kelkal, who was brought up in France, perpetrated the attack on the RER B rapid transit line at Saint-Michel station in Paris on July 25, 1995, killing 8 and injuring 148. But members of networks from other countries can also find opportunities to spend time in the West, as the members of al-Qaeda who attacked the Twin Towers in New York had done in Germany. For the intelligence services, the task of identifying each of these two types of terrorists raises different problems.

The need for information about these terrorists, homegrown or not, about how and why they embrace ideologies advocating violence, and about the forms of action they take, has in great part made radicalization a key notion for understanding the stages in the formation of terrorists.

A TINY MINORITY

In Western and even Islamic societies, the phenomenon of radicalization affects only a minority, and a tiny one at that. Many may embrace a radical ideology, and many can spiral into violence for economic or social reasons (delinquency, crimes of passion), but few combine the two dimensions and make violence a means of self-expression. Governments do so when they adhere to a supremacist ideology (the superiority of one race or social group over others) or set themselves up as representatives of a privileged class (the working class, in the case of the Soviet Union under Stalin) or of a nation (Hitler's Germany, for example, where National Socialism led to radical nationalism). As I define it, however, the term "radicalization" does not encompass the state. It includes only movements from below, instigated by individuals or groups advocating an extremist ideology and resorting to violent action. The notion of radicalization has elective affinities with that of terrorism but is distinguished from it in that the focus is on the terrorists' motivations—on the types of organizations that shape their thinking and which they shape in turn.

Only a very small minority of people become radicalized, both in the West (I am thinking of jihadists but also of those on the violent far right, such as the Norwegian Anders Breivik) and in other parts of the world. In the Muslim world, jihadist movements may enjoy the sympathy of a greater or lesser number of people, but jihadists in the strict sense of the term are very few in number, even in Pakistan.

In the West, the number of murders and assassinations imputable to jihadism, associated with an extremist version of Islam, or to terrorism in general, including those by the far right or far left, is quite limited if one considers the period after July 2005. The attacks of September 11, 2001, killed 2,973 and wounded 6,291, not counting

4

the 19 hijackers who flew the planes into the Twin Towers and the Pentagon. The attacks by jihadists on March 11, 2004, in the suburban trains of Madrid killed 191 and injured 1,858. Those of July 7, 2005, in the London Underground and in a bus, killed 52, in addition to the 4 suicide bombers, and injured some 700. Since that time (before November 2014), only Anders Breivik's attack on July 22, 2011 (77 dead, 151 wounded) killed more than 50 victims in a Western nation.

Europol statistics for France and Europe for the years 2011 and 2012 show that jihadist terrorism has been insignificant there in recent years, in terms of the number of attacks and of persons arrested, though the figures vary a great deal from one year to the next, as does the number of people killed.

Nevertheless, public anxiety is directed primarily toward radical Islamists. Corsican and Basque separatism (less and less) and far-right terrorism (the Breivik case or the far right in Greece, Germany, and even France) do not raise as many fears as radical Islamism. There is obviously an anxiety linked to jihadism, which translates into excessive media coverage, itself linked to the intensity of the fear experienced by the public. Jihadist radicalization is not placed on the same footing as regional separatism or political extremism in Europe, because the danger it represents is not perceived in the same way: separatism is considered internal to society, whereas radical Islamism is experienced as external, Islam still being, for the vast majority, a non-European religion. From that standpoint, domestic Islamist terrorists are even more worrying: they embody not only a threat but a betrayal of European identity. The disproportion between the real danger and the perceived danger can also be attributed to the development of jihadism in the Muslim world, the misdeeds committed there (carnage, a high number of victims) being transposed to the domestic scene. It could just as easily be argued that jihadism has in great part been neutralized, precisely because of the increased

Table 1. Terrorist Attacks in France and in Europe, 2011–2012

		France	Europe
2011	Number of terrorist attacks	85 separatist attacks 0 jihadist attacks	174 attacks recorded in 7 countries (France, Germany, Great Britain, Spain, Italy, Denmark, Greece), with no successful jihadist attacks
	Number of people arrested for terrorism	172, 46 for jihadism, 126 for separatism	484, 122 for religious terrorism
	Number of people convicted of terrorism	45	316
2012	Number of terrorist attacks	125, 4 by jihadists, 121 by separatists	219, 6 by jihadists, 167 by separatists, 18 by the far left, 2 by the far right
	Number of people arrested for terrorism	186, 91 for jihadism, 95 for separatism	537, 159 for jihadism, 257 for separatism, 24 on the far left 10 on the far right 87 unspecified

Source: Europol Te-Sat 2012 and 2013.

vigilance of the intelligence services and law enforcement; the relatively low number of jihadist attacks in Europe may be due to the concentration of these agencies on that type of terrorism. In any event, the symbolic dimension of jihadist terrorism is fundamental. Mohamed Merah killed seven people, including three children, but the impact of these deaths is not measured by their number, and the feeling of insecurity that resulted was much higher than in the case of far-left or far-right terrorism in Europe. The "inhuman" character of Islamist radicalism also comes into play, as well as its motivations, which are difficult to fathom: the declaration of an intent to kill "heretics" contrasts sharply with the motivations of other terrorists, grounded in the world here below (class struggle for the far-left movements, war against an invading Islam for the far right, the desire to do battle with the federal government in the United States for ultra-conservative activists).

THE NOTION OF RADICALIZATION
IN THE SOCIAL SCIENCES

Radicalization cannot be approached solely as a national security concern, though that dimension prevails in the preoccupations of nation-states. Sociologists believe it necessary to raise the question of the forms of activism within a broader perspective and to analyze the underlying motivations of extremists by inquiring, in particular, into the long-term effects of stigmatization, humiliation, and insidious forms of rejection or exclusion of which disadvantaged populations are the object in society. That dimension is often minimized in repressive or intelligence strategies, but the sociologist's role is precisely to displace the debate, which is at risk of focusing exclusively on law enforcement, and to emphasize the economic, political, and even socio-anthropological aspects of the phenomenon within an all-encompassing perspective. Radicalization must not be assessed solely within a national security context; it must become a problem entailing our understanding of society. The classic studies on terrorism raise that concern only implicitly, without focusing on it, whereas radicalization, which is attracting increased interest, designates institutional, organizational causes and also subjective forms linked to them much more explicitly than in the past. In particular, the new forms of symbolic acculturation through the Internet and mechanisms within closed groups are beginning to be understood, as is the withdrawal of individuals who "self-radicalize," severing their ties with "normal people," concealing their new allegiances from family and friends, and establishing connections through social media

(Facebook, Twitter, and so on) with people they know only via the Web. Finally, the emphasis on radicalization highlights the modalities by which people turn to violence, based on the absorption of an ideology and on decisions that may entail ambivalence and uncertainty, as when individuals subscribe to the prevailing logic of a group for fear of finding themselves once again alone and without support. Others, on the contrary, may act in a deliberate effort to cross swords with society, based on forms of subjectivization that bind them to a destiny but whose modalities were not sufficiently taken into account in classic sociological studies dealing with extremism.

The process of radicalization occurs between the short and the medium term, even extending into the long term. One does not become radicalized within a few days. The process is longer, involving "maturation" over a period of months: changes, at first imperceptible, in modes of reasoning, affectivity, and sociability with those close to the individual, who sometimes sense the enigmatic transformation without managing to understand it. The short-term effect, after an individual maturation process, or in some cases a collective one (several individuals together), may be a violent act: a hostage taking or mass murder. Once under way, radicalization also entails a mobilization of symbols, the media being called upon to fabricate the status of "negative hero," which the radicalized (Islamist extremists or secular ones, such as Breivik in Norway) quite readily adopt. That symbolic dimension, absent from the classic phenomena of extremism/radicalization (anarchists in the late nineteenth century did not seek that type of notoriety), underscores the psycho-anthropological aspect of the new forms of radicalization.

Until the 1980s (before the fall of the Berlin Wall in 1989), radicalization availed itself of a well-defined ideological corpus supported by nation-states, and the bipolar world eliminated the "psychologization" of radicality. Psychological factors played a role, but everything conspired to limit their effects: the existence of a well-established terminology, issues well circumscribed within each bloc, and institutionalized forms of sociability making it very unlikely that individuals would "go wilding" on their own. At present, however, radicalization does not result solely from an objective situation (the marginalization in Europe of the descendants of immigrants from Muslim countries, the situation of conflict in the Muslim world, the pro-Israeli policy of the United States vis-à-vis the Palestinians, and so forth); the purely subjective dimension is also assuming greater importance. It is that dimension that a sociological and anthropological approach can bring to light. The questions of knowledge that arise when the social sciences consider radicalization extend far beyond the national security perspective of intelligence and law enforcement agencies.

It should be noted that the field delimited by the word *terrorism* covers in great part that of radicalization.[3] Studies of terrorism are intended to explain sociologically, politically, or in general terms the tendency of certain groups to use ideologized violence (Wieviorka 1988). Such studies include the state within their purview, whereas state terrorism is excluded from the notion of radicalization, which focuses on small groups. When considering terrorism, sociologists are not as interested in the fact that individuals become radicalized and opt for violence (though that may be part of the overall analysis) as in the political and social significance of the phenomenon. The role of individuals and their mental states is subordinated to the entire social, political, and international dynamic. In the case of radicalization, by contrast, sociologists are sensitive to the modalities of individual subjectivization and group membership, as well as to the interaction between the group and the individual, in a play of mirrors where individual psychology has a role along with the group dynamic, the leader's charisma, and the intensity of attachment to that leader and to the ideals professed by the group. Transverse links with radicalization can also be found in the notion of "the masses" or the "crowd" and in the complex relationship, described by Sigmund

9

Freud, Elias Canetti, and Gustave Le Bon, that such collectivities maintain with their leader.

The notion of radicalization, however, stems primarily from the specificity of radical Islamism, and it highlights the sectarian and antisocial character of most of the groups that embrace that vision. They do so in the name of an ideology wherein religion plays a direct role, not in the name of a secular ideology rooted in mythic personifications of immanent human collectivities: the "people," the "proletariat," "the white race," or "the Aryan." The notion of radicalization may provide an explanation, in social scientific terms, for what seems to be a strange phenomenon (at least for the West): the return of the religious in a violent form. The ultimate objective of those involved in Islamist terrorism is to inflict death on the enemy or to submit to death themselves, which bestows the status of martyrdom. There is something unprecedented in that phenomenon and in the number of those who embrace holy death (martyrdom) to promote a type of struggle and to defend issues that seemed to have been superannuated by the Enlightenment. In Europe, and particularly in France, there is a general acceptance of what the people decide about the social and the political, and God has no place in those realms. Voices are now being heard that may call into question the sociology of secularization and the approach of the social sciences, which is confined solely to the world here below. The analysis of radicalization has the task of providing, among other things, an immanent explanation for issues proclaimed to be transcendental by those involved, who make reference to a religiosity that, even in the 1960s, still seemed largely anachronistic, even archaic. Within the perspective of the social sciences, a theory of radicalization must explain the resilience of deadly forms of religiosity (the glorification of death by self-styled martyrs) and other modes of expression that could be called neo-archaic—an oxymoron whose content is far from exhausted—wherein the inversion of life-affirming ideals occurs through religion. The challenge issued to the social sciences is to explain that type of religiosity without appealing to theology: an immanent and not transcendental meaning must be found, in sociological and anthropological terms, for that theological vision.

In the West, moreover, radicalization on a massive scale comes about in the context of what is called "deinstitutionalization." Many institutions have been weakened or even obliterated, hobbling entire strata of the population. Such is the case for labor unions and for political parties such as the Communist Party, whose disappearance or marginalization has made economic and social integration by the lower strata of society extremely difficult. As long as the Communist Party was strong in France and Italy, it conferred a distinct social identity and an associated dignity on many workers and their children. The decline of the Communist Party has occurred within a historical conjuncture when social advancement is no longer possible for a large portion of the lower classes, who are reduced to economic exclusion. When exclusion is accompanied by stigmatization, an explosive mix can result. Groups that are both mistreated and stripped of the political means for expressing their social situation have a tendency either to retreat into passivity and silence, with an increased risk of engaging in criminal behavior, or to express their revolt through violence, radical Islamism being one of these modes of expression. The imaginary mode of operation of those who embrace that type of action aggravates the situation. The Islamic referent triggers a mechanism that can lead to extremes: the symbols of jihad (holy war) are mobilized, and activist groups from other parts of the world come to play an exacerbating role, especially via the Web.

In the Muslim world, the neoliberal policies called *Infitah* ("opening"), conducted from the 1970s on, have called into question an implicit contract: acceptance of authoritarianism in exchange for social benefits. Jihadism is another expression of that questioning, in which protest, but also the visible failure of autocratic nationalism and the

11

myth of a return to the roots of Islam, gives rise to a new, antimodern utopianism.

In any event, there is a relation between jihadism and social exclusion: the exclusion in Europe of the children and grandchildren of immigrants, who are reduced to marginality, and in the Muslim world of the modernized social strata, especially the middle classes, the self-proclaimed spokespersons for the strata reduced to destitution or helplessness (*mostadh'af*). A number of educated young people have not found employment and feel exiled from society by despotic and corrupt powers. Another factor is the disappearance of the bipolar world, in which ideology played an essential role for both sides. Islam has now partly taken on the role once played by utopian versions of collective salvation, whether Marxist (the class struggle will put an end to social injustice) or liberal (the market is the miracle solution to every problem).

In the sociological literature, radicalization is often considered the articulation between an extremist ideology and a more or less organized violent act (Bronner 2009). Violent acts without a radical ideology take several forms (criminality, violence connected to some degree to a situation or a mental disturbance, and so on); conversely, for many people, radical ideology may remain at the purely theoretical level and not lead to violent acts. It is when a conjunction occurs between the two that it is possible to speak of radicalization in the strict sense of the term.

Radicalization culminating in mass violence was not possible before the advent of new technologies. With the invention of dynamite, photography, and telegraphy, extremist groups, such as the Russian anarchists in the late nineteenth century, were able to devise actions that could kill a fairly large number of people and spread the news to the whole world. Likewise, the desire to seek self-affirmation in death by accepting martyrdom within jihadism has led to new forms of action. Suicide bombers consent to sacrifice themselves, taking with them dozens or even hundreds of victims (Cook 2010; Kepel 2003). Social media are called on to disseminate the news on a vast scale in order to intimidate "the enemy" and encourage "friends."

Radicalization is marked by the linkage between a radical ideological vision and the implacable will to implement it.[4] There is, then, a twofold radicality, which neither of the components possesses alone: first, extremist ideology and, second, extremist acts inspired by that ideology but having their own specificity. Once the act is set in motion, it follows its own trajectory, given the necessities governing its realization and the unpredictability of events.

It should be noted that radicalization is not confined to Muslim countries or to extremist groups that embrace Islam in the West or elsewhere (India, Thailand, China). It is possible to become radicalized by other ideologies, secular or religious, almost anywhere in the world—for example, neo-Nazism or neo-Fascism in Europe, environmental extremism (ecoterrorism, one of the branches of deep ecology), "pro-life" ideologies leading to the violent rejection of abortion, and antihomosexual views (which have led to killings in the United States, Russia, and Muslim countries). Radical Islam, however, has been at the center of the overwhelming majority of studies on radicalization, not only because of the impact of the September 11 attacks and the turbulent history of the Middle East, but also because Islamist attacks are viewed in Europe and the United States as a much greater threat than those resulting from other forms of terrorism (though the statistics do not bear out this view). The symbolic dimension of Islamist terrorism is thus fundamental to the West's perception.

Several stages in the process of radicalization can be distinguished: preradicalization, identification with the radical movements, absorption of the extremist doctrines, and finally direct involvement in violent acts (Silber and Bhatt 2007; McCauley and Moskalenko 2008).

Theories of radicalization focus on cultural, political, psychosocial, and international factors, but also on factors internal to the radicalized groups and on the role of the media and Internet social networks. Emphasis is placed on the disruption of social bonds[5] and on political factors and how they are perceived by the radicalized (Crenshaw 2005). Some analyses concentrate on the specific traits of small groups that close themselves off from the external world; in such cases, radicalization occurs through isolation in a sectarian organization possessing a strong identity at odds with that of the larger society. Those in the underground group break off from society and from the real, retaining only their bonds to other members of the group, who are themselves cut off from others and stand against the outside world. In living in that state of secrecy, in a bubble, seeking an ideal of "purity" that can degenerate into violence against others, they become increasingly radicalized.[6]

Involvement in violent acts may be individual, carried out by a "lone wolf." Or, once the individual has taken the step of joining a group, it may result as much from interaction with its members and from isolation from the larger society—linked especially to strategies associated with life underground[7]—as from the group's internal dynamic. The group engaged in violent acts is under threat, which leads to a shared identity that reinforces the social dynamics, favoring overall cohesiveness at the expense of individual rational judgment. As a result, modes of violent action may become all the more attractive, in that the group gradually loses any sense of reality by virtue of its sectarian isolation. Not every sectarian group becomes violent, obviously, nor do all its members become radicalized, but if the ingredients of radicalization are present, being confined together can favor the recourse to violence.

For some individuals, Internet connections with radicalized groups play an essential role: both the individual and the "group of friends" thus constituted develop violent reflexes, with imitation and the hero cult amplifying their antagonistic attitude toward society. In these groups, leadership takes a decentralized and nonhierarchical form (Sageman 2004; Leiken and Brooke 2006). According to this view, networks weaken the role of personalities and give rise to leaderless radical groups (Sageman 2008).

That assessment can be disputed, however, especially given the development of new forms of radicalization in prison and also on the street, where the charismatic leader plays an undeniable role in enlisting other individuals, sometimes easily influenced or psychologically fragile, within very small (two- or three-member) groups (Khosrokhavar 2013).

Some specialists attempt to explain radicalization in terms of the interaction among the decision-making processes of terrorist elites, the motivations of mere "foot soldiers," and the organizational problems associated with finding and socializing recruits.[8] These factors are said to contribute toward radicalization through the cumulative effects of interactions within a closed group.

Others emphasize cultural orientations and the important role they play in the context of globalization. The cultural approach introduces notions such as the "culture of violence" (Juergensmeyer 2003) or "violent subcultures" within society. In addition, groups that develop an intense sense of victimhood because of their stigmatization or their history ("internal colonialism" or any other grievance against the larger society) can become involved in so-called legitimate violence against others.

Another set of radicalization studies focuses more particularly on religious ideologies. They note that European Muslim communities resulting from immigration tend to favor rigid interpretations of Islam (especially in organizations such as the Tablighi Jamaat and Salafism), which might explain their sympathy for radical Islamism (Coolsaet 2005). These theories do not explain, however, why extremist versions of other religions no longer lead to "holy war."

Finally, rational-choice theories attempt to propose a "rational" view of radical action. From their standpoint, terrorist action is a conscious choice based on a well-thought-out decision about the strategy best able to achieve fixed sociopolitical goals, especially when the adversary is far superior militarily and leaves the group no chance whatever for an eventual victory in a classic war (see Gambetta 2005). In choosing the terrorist option, then, al-Qaeda would be making a rational choice, given its relative weight when compared to that of the United States and, more broadly, the West, and would adopt a strategy giving it room for maneuvering that would be unavailable in a classic struggle. The radicality of those involved thus has a dimension that extends beyond any emotional consideration and belongs to a strategic calculation possessing its own "rationality."

In the new forms of radicalization, the effect of the imagined community to which jihadists belong is fundamental. In identifying with a "new Ummah" (a warm and mythically homogeneous Muslim community, whose existence they hope and pray for), they attempt to mark themselves off from the cold society in which they live, where *anomie* (literally, "without law," lack of membership in a group that confers identity) goes hand in hand with stigmatization and social insignificance.

My point of view embraces a sociology of subjects within a context of globalization, where radicalized individuals conduct themselves in conformance with a threefold orientation:

- First, as humiliated individuals. Such is the case for the young people in the impoverished outskirts of French cities, known as the *banlieues*, or in the ghettoized neighborhoods of Great Britain, or for young Palestinians humiliated by Israel, but also for young people brought up in the Middle East, often with scientific training, who find no work or feel marginalized by authoritarian regimes. Whether these individuals belong to the lower or to the middle classes, they criticize the system for reducing them to insignificance, for humiliating them by marginalizing them politically and economically.

- Second, as victimized individuals. Humiliation, frustration, social and economic exclusion, and racism are experienced within an imaginary structure that gives individuals the half-real, half-fictive impression of being without a future, of facing closed doors, in short, a sense of the internalized ghetto. Those who passively endure that situation may fall into criminality or violence on an individual basis, but those who revolt and seek to act do so by ideologizing their internal experience: they expand their hatred of "non-Muslims" by adopting a jihadist vision. Islam proposes an activist alternative that far-left ideologies are no longer able to provide.

- Third, as members of a group under assault, namely, the neo-Ummah, which has no equivalent in historically constituted Muslim communities (the Muslim Ummah). That sense of belonging leads individuals to overcome their stigmatization and provides them with a new identity. They are "born again"; their status vis-à-vis society is turned on its head, and they become its implacable enemies. Previously of inferior social status—as immigrants or the children of immigrants, as Palestinians trapped in the stifling neighborhoods of Gaza, or as Egyptians living in insalubrious neighborhoods—they become heroes of Islam, now characterized as the "religion of the oppressed." With respect to the external world they intend to combat, they assume the status of negative heroes: the more they are feared, despised, and rejected by that world, which is

portrayed in stark terms, the more glory they will attract.
They are henceforth heroes for all who share their credo,
notorious public enemies for everyone else. The narcissistic
dimension combines with the "rational" dimension via the
media and the jihadists' own experience as "media heroes."
They will be known throughout the world; they will be
aggrandized and glorified by the media, which, however,
are on the adversary's side. For example, Mohamed Merah,
the perpetrator of shootings in Toulouse and Montauban,
wore a movie camera around his neck to film his acts and
have them broadcast on television stations worldwide.
Zacarias Moussaoui, while on trial for conspiring in the
attack of September 11, delivered a cruel speech in court in
May 2006, designed to insult the families of the victims,
knowing full well that, in sparking the indignation of
Americans and further tainting his image, he was at the
same time increasing his global notoriety. That "negative
celebrity" is fundamental in the subjectivization of
those becoming radicalized in our time, jihadists in
particular but also someone like Anders Breivik, the
Norwegian far-right terrorist who perpetrated the slaughter
of July 22, 2011. Breivik "advertised" his ideology by
distributing electronically, on the same day as the attacks, a
document in which he championed his "cultural conserva-
tism," ultranationalism, Islamophobia, antifeminism,
"white nationalism," and Zionism, and his opposition to
multiculturalism, "Eurabia,"[9] and Muslims, who he said
ought to be expelled from Europe to preserve Christianity.
He sent his 1,518-page *Manifesto 2083*—written not in
Norwegian but in English, so as to be accessible to the
whole world—to more than a thousand people and also
posted many messages on the website www.document.no,

all with the aim of disseminating information worldwide and practicing globalized seduction. For him, the attacks were part of the publicity surrounding his plan for a new Europe.

These three dimensions belong to the context of globalization, and radicalized individuals have internalized them perfectly. Terrorist actions and the global media coverage of them are now inextricably linked. The symbolic dimension of information, but also of intimidation and fascination, and the conditioning of the adversary through the shock of images (producing a sense of helplessness) go hand in hand with the brutality of the act itself: the radicalized subject acts as much to attract attention as to cause damage.

Furthermore, people become radicalized when they feel a profound sense of the injustice inflicted on them and on the group to which they believe they belong, and when they feel that a reformist attitude cannot remedy that injustice. Not every feeling of intolerable injustice necessarily gives rise to radicalization, but all radicalization presupposes such a feeling in its core group. The sense of injustice may be connected to everyday life (repression of the Chechens by the Russian army, of the Palestinians by the Israeli army, or of the Kashmiri by the Indian army, to cite only a few examples), and a radicalization of the nationalist type then results. But the sense of injustice may also extend, on the basis of lived experience or by proxy, to the total vision of the world of the subject being radicalized. Young French people of Maghrebi descent, placed in a position of social marginality, transpose the Palestinians' experience vis-à-vis the Israeli army to their own in the French *banlieues* whenever they tangle with the police. That imaginary displacement is not necessarily grounded in reality (the police in France are not the Israeli army in Palestine), but it is nonetheless fueled by imitation and ultimately expands to include all the individual's social and political relationships. To pursue the example already cited, young people from the French *banlieues* become radicalized in believing that Islam is under assault by the West, citing their own relations with law enforcement (Muslims mistreated by the police, Islamophobia) and the examples of Bosnia, Afghanistan, Iraq, and Mali, to conclude that France oppresses Muslims throughout the world in collusion with the United States. As a result, they fancy themselves the saviors of Islam and opt for jihad, inside France (like Mohamed Merah) or outside it (as in Farid Benyettou's group). In radicalization, the imagination, subjectivization, imitation, subjective proxies, and a sense of humiliation play very large roles. Outcast French young people of North African descent put themselves in the shoes of Palestinians or, more generally, of Muslim Arabs humiliated by Israel or by the West. Young Pakis[10] imagine they are Kashmiri oppressed by the Indian army. Young Chechens rebel against oppression by the Russian army or, in a manner even further removed from the real, they may by proxy radicalize themselves against their host country (the United States for the Tsarnaev brothers, who perpetrated the Boston Marathon attacks) and declare themselves heralds of Islam in the fierce and ruthless struggle against an oppressive America.

Radicalization thus assumes imaginary dimensions, based on images cobbled together on the Internet or seen on television; by means of friendships, close or remote, established on the Web or in prison; or in contact with individuals already radicalized or in revolt against the unjust treatment they have received because of their religious affiliation (Islam) or ethnic identity (Arab, black, or mixed race).

In anthropological terms, radicalization has an undeniably political dimension, but it is expressed sub- or superpolitically (Wieviorka 1988). Subpolitically, radicalized individuals express their rancor and desire for change by responding emotionally and engaging in violence, rather than seeking solutions that could find political expression. Violence can in fact lead to solutions, but it often exacerbates tensions and has a counterproductive effect, radicalizing the adversary instead of encouraging negotiation. Superpolitically, a frenzied utopianism can prompt radicalization. Among jihadists, the utopia, a universal neocalifate taking root in every Islamic society and beyond, is metapolitical, as unrealizable as a classless society.

The political, then, is ill-served within the very logic of radicalization, especially when its aim is a supernational or transnational utopia. Robert Pape (2006) indicates that the overwhelming majority of suicide attacks can be attributed to the presence of a foreign army on national soil, not to religious motivations. My intent, in fact, is to introduce a difference between two types of utopianism. The first is limited, often entailing precise grievances and reasonable demands. Nationalism, including its Islamo-nationalist form, is the most widespread model. The ideal pursued—the constitution of a nation—is concrete. Such is the case for the Palestinians, the Kashmiri, and the Chechens. If that utopianism runs up against so many obstacles that subjects eventually despair of seeing it realized, however, another sort of utopianism takes shape, one I call frenzied, which is radicalization of the transnational type. But the second model of utopianism can also exist independently of the first, without necessarily being the consequence of radicalization. In the first case, Robert Pape's hypothesis is valid: one of the means to fight a foreign army occupying a territory for a relatively long period of time, when there is a glaring imbalance of forces, is to organize suicide operations. By contrast, when utopianism is frenzied—for example, in the struggle against imperialism in its entirety or for the establishment of a classless society or a global caliphate, as championed by al-Qaeda—the realization of the goal is inconceivable for the foreseeable future. In Europe, radical Islamism and attempted suicide attacks have nothing to do with an armed presence in the native country of the perpetrators, who are for the most part homegrown terrorists. They have two grievances: humiliation at home (in Europe) and assaults on Muslim countries abroad, in conformance with a model in which imaginary constructions are of key importance. Radicalization is of a different nature in limited utopianism and in its frenzied form.

In the radicalization process, the two most widespread feelings are humiliation and despair, coupled with the desire to inflict an even more profound humiliation on the adversary and the conviction that it will be possible to realize a utopia based on a "theology of wild hope," which justifies the irenic vision of a future indeterminate in time. Despair and humiliation can dictate violent behaviors (radicalization) without necessarily being accompanied by the theology of wild hope, but the desire to inflict greater humiliation on the adversary is omnipresent in all forms of radicalization. Radicalized Islamists are motivated by the idea that if they are patient, and if they also engage in jihadist action, God will intervene to establish a universal theocracy. The other facet of their ideology is the aspiration to inflict humiliation on the arrogant West and, beyond it, on a world hostile to the ideals they profess. That ideology is at once of this world (humiliate, demean, and fight the enemy ferociously here and now) and beyond this world (await divine intervention to annihilate the more powerful enemy).

1

The History of Radicalization

THE ASSASSINS, A FIRST ATTEMPT AT RADICALIZATION

Several periods can be distinguished in the history of radicalization, as that term is understood here, that is, as it applies to small groups. According to some, the Assassins of the eleventh century embodied the first systematic attempt at radicalization in the premodern world. Hassan-i Sabbah, who ruled a small state with its center at the Alamut Fortress in Iran, about sixty miles from the present-day capital, Tehran, founded a sectarian group composed of believers who were ready to sacrifice themselves on his order in assassinating those he designated. That secret society, which embraced Ismaʿīlism, a minority branch of Shia Islam, was formidably effective against Sabbah's political adversaries, notably the Seljuk vizier Nizām al-Mulk, who was killed in 1092. The indoctrination that took place and the combination of a radical, sectarian ideology with violent acts amount to terrorism as it is currently understood. According to legend, Sabbah used hashish to keep his disciples in a trance state and to give them a foretaste of the pleasures of paradise, in the garden located within the walls of Alamut Fortress, his place of residence.

ANARCHIST TERRORISM IN THE NINETEENTH
AND EARLY TWENTIETH CENTURIES

In the modern world, the first outbursts of sporadic violence were those of the new workers' movement in Europe in the late eighteenth century, before it established an organization and constructed an alternative plan for society, sponsored by utopian Communists such as Marx and Engels. Intermittently, artisans mounted attacks on the machines that had dispossessed them of their traditional work, or on the police, who prevented them from forming organized groups. The first labor unions often came into being under threat from the police but also from militias controlled by management. Groups of radical intellectuals formed in countries such as Tsarist Russia, where the authorities often fought on two fronts, against their own reactionary partisans and against the world of intellectuals and workers in the making. These radicals played an undeniable role in radicalizing large swaths of societies undergoing modernization (intellectuals, the middle classes, scientists, and so on). Of particular note were the nihilists, the Decembrists, and the many free-floating intellectuals who threw their lot in with those who opposed autocracy. They supported the new working class emerging in Russia and advocated proletarian revolution, legitimizing "popular" violence against the authoritarianism of the reigning powers and the persistence of serfdom (it was not suppressed until 1861, and then only imperfectly). The Decembrist insurrection of 1825 failed, and repressive measures were taken against its leaders. The brutality of the repression radicalized new groups, who rejected the possibility of reform within the Russian autocratic regime. In particular, the Russian anarchist organization Narodnaya Volya (Will of the People) developed in the last quarter of the nineteenth century; its most noteworthy act was the assassination of Emperor Alexander II in March 1881.

In the nineteenth century, anarchism became the vehicle for revolutionary violence against capitalism, the powers that supported it, and the archaic autocracies of Europe. Russian anarchists committed violent acts—"propaganda of the deed" to use their term—grounded in an ideological vision that rejected legalism. Combined with written or oral propaganda, these actions challenged legal mechanisms while promoting "permanent revolt" as the only path to revolution. Granted, the failure of the 1848 revolution almost everywhere in Europe and Latin America, and its repression by the authoritarian regimes in place—like the failure of the Commune in 1871, which culminated in the army's execution of thirty thousand Communards—drove to despair a large portion of the intellectuals and activists who had hoped for a peaceful and legal transition to socialism. Radicalization of the anarchist groups came about through the constitution of closed groups ruled by a dictatorship of the collective. Hence one could join Narodnaya Volya, but it was forbidden to leave it, on pain of death. Likewise, every member of the executive committee of Narodnaya Volya "solemnly swore to devote his energies to the revolution, to forget for its sake all blood ties, personal sympathies, love, and friendship; to give his life freely; to have nothing that belonged to him exclusively; to renounce his individual will" (Cannac 1961: 149). This was similar to the commitment made by the members of Hassan-i Sabbah's sect. They, however, thought they would go to paradise by killing or intimidating those designated by the *dā'ī*, or guide, whereas members of the anarchist group executed the orders of the Committee in the name of the people in chains. In the first case, the sacred was religious, in the second secular, but the source of both was untouchable, indisputable. Propaganda of the deed included, in particular, terrorist acts, punitive expeditions, sabotage, acts of guerilla warfare, and other types of violent action (Vareilles 2005).

Many assassination attempts were organized by anarchists at the turn of the twentieth century, and several were successful: the assassination of French president Sadi Carnot on June 24, 1894; of Spanish prime minister Antonio Cánovas del Castillo in August 1897 (in reprisal for the torture and execution of anarchists in Barcelona); of the empress of Austria on September 10, 1898; of the king of Italy, Umberto I, on July 29, 1900; of U.S. president William McKinley on September 14, 1901; and of Marius Plateau, one of the founding members of the far-right anti-Semitic nationalist group Action Française, on January 22, 1923. Assassination attempts against Emperor William I of Germany, Georges Clémenceau in France, and Benito Mussolini in Italy failed.

On the whole, the anarchist movement attacked government authorities, not only to influence public opinion but also to avenge the repression of its members or to mobilize the working class against the bourgeoisie. The revolutionaries who carried out the attacks came from several different European countries, giving rise to an international organization of violent agents even before the political union of Europe. In several of its aspects, the anarchist movement resembled al-Qaeda: in its transnational character, the all-encompassing nature of its aims (general grievances against the Western world as a whole, rejection of lawfulness, the ideological legitimization of violence), and in its members' devotion to the cause even unto death. National borders were no longer a barrier. An action could take place in Russia, France, the United States, Italy, or other countries, though Asia was not a target and Latin America was little affected.

Anarchist violence accompanied systematic violence on a global scale: the working classes were reduced to destitution, and repression by the ruling authorities was extremely harsh.[1] Al-Qaeda and opposition jihadist groups now invoke the fate of Muslims, especially the Sunni, who according to them are being repressed by the Shia with the complicity of Western Crusaders; or they speak of the Palestinian question and Israeli repression. A backdrop of institutionalized violence lies behind terrorist acts, especially when a radical ideology informs the fight of those who use terrorism to compensate for their military weakness. Radicalization results when individuals perceive violence and interpret it along ideological lines, becoming violent themselves.

THE VIOLENT FAR LEFT IN THE 1970s–1990s

Long after the anarchism of the late nineteenth and early twentieth centuries, in the 1970s and 1980s, the "years of lead," a new type of violence emerged in Europe and the United States, based on radical far-left ideologies. Three European countries were the primary victims: France, by the Action Directe movement; Italy, by the Red Brigades (Brigate Rosse); and Germany, by the Red Army Faction (Rote Armee Fraktion, or RAF). In the United States, radical groups, such as the Weathermen and the Symbionese Liberation Army (SLA), mounted attacks on various targets, reviving the practices of violent anarchists in the late nineteenth century. These movements arose in reaction to a complex sociopolitical climate. On the one hand, dictatorships were installed on the right and far right, especially in African countries (the reign of Sékou Touré in Guinea, the hard line taken by Hassan II's regime in Morocco, and others). In Latin America, the military coup d'état of Augusto Pinochet in Chile in September 1973 put an end to the democratic experiment of Salvador Allende, and various dictatorships collaborated in Operation Condor to liquidate opponents, waging a "dirty war" in which even the bodies disappeared. On the other hand, the end of the revolutionary mission of parties identified with the working class and their embrace of electoral politics (especially Communist parties in France and Italy after World War II) led to the sense, for some on the revolutionary left, that it had been abandoned. In France, despite the burgeoning of frenzied utopianism in May 1968, elections solidified the right's

27

power. In Italy, the Communist Party, on the strength of its electoral success, renounced the path of revolution and clearly chose the ballot box over force of arms.

The Italian Red Brigades was the largest radical movement, both in the number of members (more than a thousand) and in the number of revolutionary organizations involved. Its most notorious action was the kidnapping of Aldo Moro in 1978. After a fifty-five-day captivity, during which time the government refused to negotiate, the former leader of the Italian government was executed. The Red Brigades was founded by Alberto Franceschini and Renato Curcio in October 1970 with the aim of resuming the armed struggle of the Communist left, which the party had abandoned after World War II. Red Brigades partisans began "armed propaganda" or "armed struggle," using acts of violence, such as assassinations, shootings in the legs of targeted persons, and the forcible detention of agents of the state (police, magistrates) but also of journalists, politicians, and others. They also murdered labor activists, such as, in January 1979, Guido Rossa, who had turned in a worker distributing their tracts. In 1981 the movement split into several subgroups, one of which joined the Red Army Faction in the Federal Republic of Germany in 1988. During the 1980s, most of the first-generation members of the brigade abandoned armed struggle. A second generation surfaced and committed violent acts, in particular the murder in March 2002 of a consultant to the Italian government. In 2005, five members of the Red Brigades were sentenced to life in prison for that act. In February 2007, fifteen presumed terrorists were arrested as they were planning attacks, according to the police; the group was composed of young recruits but also of veterans. Six people suspected of belonging to the New Red Brigades were arrested in June 2009 and charged with planning attacks on the G8 summit in Italy. Under François Mitterrand's presidency, in view of the sympathy of the country's intellectuals, France agreed not to extradite the three hundred or so members who had taken refuge on its soil, provided they agree not to plan violent acts. An exception was made, however, for those who had committed murder (Laske 2012). In 1981, 1,523 people close to the Red Brigades, having been charged with terrorism, were incarcerated in Italy. The Soviet Union provided logistical support to the movement, and certain of its members lived secretly in Czechoslovakia. Some people say that the Red Brigades was also infiltrated by the CIA or even by the Italian secret services.

The radicalization of members of the Red Brigades conforms, in the first place, to forces at work in Italy, where individuals, especially from the middle classes, declare themselves representatives of the working class and aspire to lead the class struggle with weapons in hand, a fight the Italian Communist Party renounced when it became an electoral force in the country. That self-proclaimed commitment to represent a group considered sacred can also be found in present-day jihadist movements: their members say they are the authentic defenders of Islam, supposedly flouted by the traditional ulema (councils of Muslim legal scholars), by so-called Islamic governments (Saudi Arabia), and by other powers in the Muslim world, which are accused of being in the pay of global idolatry (taqut), alias the imperialism of the Crusaders or of Zionism. Radicalization occurs all the more easily in that this sense of being the true representatives of a sacred order (the working class, Islam, the West) is profoundly rooted in the minds of the group's members and legitimized by radical ideology, which leads to acts of violence. Over time, the organization must evolve if it is to succeed in transmitting to young people the message of struggle and to continue its actions by recruiting new members. In the same way, jihadist organizations such as al-Qaeda bridge the generation gap with a pitch whose lexicon hardly changes but whose tenor is adjusted to fit the new situation (the relationship between leaders and members and between different groups embracing the same ideology, changes in the political and international context, and so on).

By the 1990s, the Red Brigades movement was showing signs that it was running out of steam, first because its members had been arrested, and second because violent action had lost its legitimacy in the Italian political arena.

The name Action Directe (Direct Action) comes from anarchist theory. Members of that group—estimated at about 180—claimed responsibility for more than eighty violent acts in France between 1979 and 1987, which killed a dozen and injured twenty-six (Dartnell 1995). Banned by the French state in 1982, the movement has since that time been considered a terrorist organization. Its last members, arrested and tried in 1987, were convicted of the assassinations of General René Audran, of other leading cadres in the army, of Georges Besse, CEO of the automobile manufacturer Renault, and of eminent members of French management. They were also found guilty of multiple assaults, notably attacks on the offices of Interpol and the Western European Union. The movement was divided between anarchist and Marxist-Leninist factions, the first of these being close to the German Red Army Faction. In 1979 it turned into a guerrilla organization, which claimed responsibility for attacks on imperialist capitalism, the state, and big business and procured arms and explosives through theft and armed robbery. After Mitterrand was elected president of France in 1981, the organization split into two groups: one abandoned the revolutionary struggle while still committing anti-Semitic attacks, and the other branch (in 1985) affiliated itself with the Red Army Faction to unify the revolutionary struggle in Europe (Savoie 2011). From 1982 to 1987, Action Directe committed several attacks targeting police officers, business leaders, and high-ranking military officers. The leaders of Action Directe were arrested in the 1980s and received long prison sentences.

The Red Army Faction (Rote Armee Fraktion, RAF), also called the Baader-Meinhof Gruppe, after its leaders Andreas Baader and Ulrike Meinhof, was a far-left German urban guerrilla warfare organization that operated in West Germany from 1970 to 1998, committing attacks, kidnappings, and assassinations. It grew out of the radicalization of the German student movement, which, in the late 1960s, opposed the arrival in Germany of the shah of Iran (May 1967) and denounced American imperialism, the Vietnam War, and the assassination of Che Guevara in Bolivia (also in 1967). Domestically, the radical left was powerless at that time against the coalition formed in December 1966 between the large right-wing parties (the Christian Democratic Union, the Christian Social Union) and the German Socialist Party (SPD). In June 1970, the publication of "Build Up the Red Army!" in the magazine *Agit 883* was the official declaration of the founding of the RAF, whose stated goal was to "promote class struggle, organize the proletariat, begin the armed resistance, build up the Red Army." Several members of the group stayed in a Fatah camp in Jordan, learning to handle arms and explosives. To meet its financial needs, the organization, like Action Directe and the Red Brigades, resorted to theft and armed robbery. Confrontations with the police, who were attempting to arrest the fifty or so members of the group, resulted in the death of two officers and a bystander. The bombings of American military installations and German public institutions in 1972 killed four and injured about thirty (Steiner and Debray 2006). The main leaders of the first generation of the RAF were arrested in June 1972 and imprisoned under inhumane conditions of isolation; several of them died under suspicious circumstances between 1976 and 1977. In April 1977, those who remained were sentenced to life in prison. A second generation followed, its members coming out of the Socialist Patients' Collective, founded in February 1970 by psychiatric patients from a private clinic in Heidelberg or recruited by the lawyers who were defending the first generation in court. There was also a third generation, with fewer than ten active members. Between its creation in 1970 and its dissolution in 1998, the movement had between sixty and eighty active members. Their activities resulted in the assassination of thirty-four people.

The three major European far-left terrorist groups were characterized by their longevity, two or three decades, by the relatively small number of members (fewer than a hundred for Action Directe and Red Army Faction, about a thousand for the Red Brigades), and by the national character of member recruitment (though alliances were attempted, between Action Directe and the RAF, for example, their impact was marginal overall). Internationalist in their inspiration (anti-imperialism, anticapitalism), these groups were national in their actions. Their will to take radical action could not be transmitted beyond two or three generations. On the whole, the fall of the Berlin Wall sounded the death knell of these groups, which were compelled to end their activities because of police repression and their own depleted resources, as well as their incapacity to train new generations. Such is not the case for jihadism, which has persisted since the 1980s without showing any sign of decline, only some changes at most.

THE DIFFERENT PHASES OF AL-QAEDA AND THE REVIVAL OF JIHADISM WITH THE ARAB SPRING

Al-Qaeda is the success story of transnational terrorism, based on a pattern of radicalization that has perpetuated itself for several generations, since the 1980s. It has become the front organization for a large number of groups that embrace its ideals, political aims, and style of struggle, in what is a more or less symbolic association. Al-Qaeda has undergone several distinct phases: relative legitimacy in the eyes of the West during the struggle against the Soviet Union in

Afghanistan (until 1989); struggle against the West, which culminated in the attacks of September 11, 2001; and finally, ever since it was weakened by American repression and a large part of its leading cadres was eliminated, a phase marked by the creation of many small groups that claim to be inspired to pursue al-Qaeda's struggle. New structures have been built up, with a number of self-sufficient groups, autonomous both financially and organizationally, with no organic connections to one another. Increasingly decentralized in their leadership, these groups place their hope in a future universal Islamic state (the neocalifate). Although some may work together on the ground, like those that have more or less unified in North Africa or in Syria and Iraq—the Islamic State of Iraq and al-Sham (ISIS), for example—that change is marked by an increasing flexibility. Groups change shape to escape international repression and attract members and sympathizers, especially on the Internet. Despite the many obstacles that stand in their way, jihadist groups, for which al-Qaeda is becoming the symbol, manage to radicalize new generations, both in the ghettos of Europe and among the new generations of modernized middle classes in the Middle East.

A new chapter of jihadism began with the Arab Spring. After Tunisian president Ben Ali fled to Saudi Arabia on January 14, 2011, and Mubarak of Egypt resigned eighteen days after the revolution that began in his country on January 25, 2011, new forms of radicalization came into being.

Initially, jihadism as a social movement experienced a crisis. Jihadists, with their martial vision and incessant violence, had not succeeded in overthrowing a single Arab regime, whereas peaceful revolutionaries had managed to take down two of the most despotic regimes of the Arab world with their bare hands. The crisis in mission was combined with an ideological crisis, which placed jihadist circles on the defensive. Nevertheless, these revolutions were also an opportunity for many radical Islamists to get out of prison, taking advantage of amnesty, a period of uncertainty, or the absence of a central power, when the doors of prisons opened a crack.

The euphoric period of the Arab Spring lasted only a few months. The economic situation deteriorated in Egypt and Tunisia, since both countries depend on tourists, who feared the political instability; that decline in tourism depleted the economic resources of the most fragile social strata. The Muslim Brotherhood in Egypt and Ennahda in Tunisia, both of which legally took power in 2012, initially had a lax attitude toward the jihadists, thinking they could convince them to embrace nonviolent behavior. Radical Islamists were therefore able to take root in Sinai during this period. Similarly, in Tunisia, jihadist Salafists succeeded in building up solid support for themselves in the poor neighborhoods in the Tunis area and in underdeveloped zones, such as Sidi Bouzid, where the revolution had begun with the suicide of Mohamed Bouazizi in December 2010. The largest jihadist organization, Ansar al-Sharia, headed by Abu Iyad (who was serving a long prison sentence under Ben Ali and received amnesty after the revolution), was thus able to gain ground. It was accused of taking part in the attack on the U.S. embassy in Tunis in September 2012 and of participating in the murder of two political leaders, Chokri Belaid in February and Mohamed Brahmi in July 2013.

In addition, Libya, a "failed state" after the overthrow of Gaddafi's regime in October 2011, continued to deteriorate, and a large part of its arsenal fell into the hands of warlords, who were able to sell weapons to different groups of jihadists, in both North Africa (Mali included) and the Middle East. Jihadist groups also developed in Yemen, with the help of President Saleh's strategy: he assisted them more or less indirectly so as to garner the support of the United States in the fight against terrorism. His departure in February 2012 did not greatly change the situation of the radical Islamists in zones where the central state is weak.

Without question, however, the place that attracts jihadists most and receives doctrinal legitimization from radical Islam is Syria. Bashar el-Assad's regime is Alawite, deviant in the eyes of many Shia, for whom Alawism is an aberration, as well as for the radical Sunni, who consider Shia Islam as a whole a heresy whose followers deserve the death penalty. Because Assad's regime is at war with a society that is largely Sunni, jihadists have found a golden opportunity to launch holy war against it in the name of their radical version of Islam. Participation in that jihad was declared an "urgent duty" (*fardh al ayn*) for every Muslim. From almost everywhere—Europe, the Middle East, North Africa, the United States, Pakistan—young people have come to fight against the ungodly regime of the Alawites; their number is estimated at about ten thousand, including a few hundred from every European country and a thousand Tunisians (see Bakker, Paulussen, and Entenmann 2013). These young people are becoming radicalized, this time on an "objective" basis: a Muslim country is suffering in the grip of a bloody regime that embraces a false religion (Alawism) and whose proponents have killed Sunni, representatives of authentic Islam. In Tunisia, Ansar al-Sharia was thus able to recruit several hundred young people, who agreed to fight against *taqut* (global idolatry, embodied by regimes complicit with the West) and to die for the holy cause of Islam. In Syria, the West and the East are uniting in jihadism. Like the Muslim countries, practically all the countries of western Europe have seen aspiring jihadists, Muslim in their upbringing or converts to Islam, leave for the Syrian war theater. The zeal for jihad attests to a state of mind oriented toward the defense of the "Muslim community," beyond national borders.

In short, the Arab Spring is behind the jihadist revival. In Syria, Yemen, and Libya, jihadists took advantage of the failure of the state (sometimes because of Western intervention, as in Libya, where NATO airpower played an undeniable role in the overthrow of Gaddafi's autocratic regime) to develop in the void thus created. Likewise, their implantation in Tunisia—along the Algerian border, in the poor neighborhoods of Tunis, and in the underdeveloped southern and central parts of the country—as well as in the Sinai Desert in Egypt was favored by the conciliatory attitude of Ennahda in Tunisia and of the Muslim Brotherhood in Egypt (until late June 2013). Both groups set out to convince the jihadist Salafists to join the legalist Islamist forces. Once jihadist groups take root in these regions, they attempt to radicalize a fringe of the local population, often those who have been left behind (the "disinherited," *mustadh'afun*), some of whom, especially in Tunisia and Egypt, subsequently turn up in Syria and later in Europe promoting a new kind of terrorism.

2

Islamist Radicalization in the Muslim World

All in all, radicalization of the younger generations in the Muslim world has been the consequence of an accumulation of Arab and Muslim humiliation and of the persistence of autocracies. The Six-Day War of 1967 and the failure of the Arab countries to defeat Israel heightened the feelings of humiliation, as did the sense that the Western world is hostile to the Arab world. Above all, the permanence of corrupt and authoritarian Arab governments has destroyed the aspirations for true citizenship (political pluralism, a more meritocratic economy) of generations who are better educated and less intimidated by shows of repression. Another factor came to bear in the 1980s: the disappearance of the welfare state established by Arab nationalists, which had ensured jobs for the younger generations in exchange for their acquiescence to authoritarianism. During the period of "liberalization," called Infitah, most of the economic and social support provided by the government gradually vanished. Moreover, Saudi Arabia, the foremost oil producer in the region, has little by little imposed its Wahhabist, puritan, and rigorist version of Islam, which shares more than one aspect of intolerance with Islamist radicalism.

Radical Islamism in the Middle East is closely connected to the despair of the younger generations, who, though better educated than in the past, are reduced to living in a schizoid world: economic conditions characteristic of the lower classes (unemployment, *hittisme*,[1] *trabendisme*[2]) but a middle-class culture and educational level. These generations have seen the failure of Arab nationalism from the Six-Day War in 1967 to the first decade of the twenty-first century.

Radical Islam inaugurated a new era of radicalization. Compared with the terrorist movements that preceded it (Russian anarchism in the nineteenth century and the Red Brigades, Action Directe, and the Red Army Faction in the 1970s and 1980s in Europe), the phenomenon is much more intense: jihadists sacrifice themselves much more readily and in much higher numbers. It is also far more widespread geographically: apart from Latin America, which has been relatively shielded, cases of autochthonous and imported jihadism can be found almost everywhere. The number of jihadists affiliated with al-Qaeda or similar organizations, or with groups claiming more or less plausibly to belong to such organizations, is much higher than that of past terrorist movements. Radical Islamism has also extended over a much longer period of time: indeed, since the 1970s and even, according to some, since the founding of the Muslim Brotherhood in 1928, it has continued to develop and shows no sign of decline. Furthermore, the random violence perpetrated in its name is of a different tenor than violence targeting specific groups (the upper administration, management, the army), characteristic of the previous movements. Finally, the salient trait of jihadism is its flexibility and its capacity to adapt to extreme situations through reorganization. Al-Qaeda and the jihadist movements are the first truly global and transnational type of terrorism to perpetuate itself over time, transform itself in the face of international and national repression by the countries concerned, and continue its struggle in multiple forms, varying them as circumstances change and constantly constructing new ones.

Three types of radicalized Islamists can be distinguished:

- Subjects from countries with a Muslim majority (the Middle East, Pakistan, Indonesia), whose grievances have intensified, shifting from protests against the current political regime to a will to establish a transnational Islamic regime (the neocalifate).
- Subjects from western Europe, North America, or Australia, where, in the last half century, Muslim minorities have become implanted. They are intent on struggling violently against Islamophobia and against assaults on Muslim countries by nations in these regions (the United States, Great Britain, France, and others) and are also driven by the will to expand the rule of Islam to the whole world, including the West (under the neocalifate, for which they hope and pray).
- Subjects from countries where Muslims are waging a national struggle against forces they perceive as occupying powers or armies. They battle the repression of the Palestinians by the Israeli army, are involved in the conflicts over Jerusalem and colonization, and oppose Western support of Israel. They fight against India, which occupies a part of Kashmir, a region Muslims would like to see either independent or annexed to Pakistan. And finally, they revolt against the Russian repression of the Chechens. In all cases, they are engaged in a nationalist conflict in the name of Islam that bestows a sacred meaning on the struggle against the occupying powers.

Unlike the situation in the Muslim world, in Europe it is primarily the young from the lower social strata who form the hard core of jihadism. Although a few members of the middle classes embrace that vision by imitation, the great majority of the radicalized are recruited in so-called tough neighborhoods or among the young of the working classes, some of them converts to Islam. These are often the children or grandchildren of immigrants from Muslim countries: the Pakis in Great Britain and those called Arabs in France, that is, young French citizens of North African descent.

Radicalization does not follow the same paths in these two worlds. In most Muslim countries, authoritarianism and corruption are rampant, whereas in Europe the democratic political system limits the scope of special privileges and their devastating effects on citizens' sense of dignity. Nevertheless, because of the widespread deterritorialization resulting from economic globalization and the increasingly large waves of migration in the world (about 214 million people a year, nearly 3 percent of the global population),[3] a small number of radicalized individuals cross the Mediterranean into Europe despite the collaboration between nation-states in the region to intercept them. Nor is there any ideological barrier: radical thought easily crosses borders, thanks to the new communication technologies (the Internet, satellite TV). Despite the porosity of borders and the resulting contagion effects, there are notable differences in the structure of radicalization, especially of the middle classes, in Europe versus the Muslim countries. In Europe, the members of the middle classes who become radicalized are a small minority, the vast majority being young people in precarious financial situations or suffering from exclusion; in the Muslim world, by contrast, the younger generations from the middle classes constitute the majority of radicalized believers.

SHIA AND SUNNI RADICALIZATION: DIFFERENCES AND SIMILARITIES

Shia is a minority branch of Islam: about 10 percent of Muslims are Shia, versus 90 percent Sunni. The Shia have long been repressed by the Sunni in the Muslim world, and their radicalization bears the marks of their history. Iran and Iraq are the only two countries in the Muslim world where the Shia are in the majority. In Iran, Shia radicalization in the 1970s led to the Islamic Revolution in 1979. Henceforth, the model of Shia radicalization underwent a profound change. It was the theocratic state that now played the leading role, whereas in the Sunni world, absent a revolutionary Islamist state, radicalization occurred in opposition to the ruling power. One consequence of the long war between Iran and Iraq (1980–1988) was the development in Iran of a type of radicalization that has a strong "dolorist" dimension, that is, it is associated with suffering. There, martyrdom has been given the starring role, especially that of Husayn, the third Shia imam, who was put to death by Calif Yazid in 680 and whose martyrdom is celebrated every year over two days, Tasu'a and Ashura, in rituals of high drama. Nevertheless, Shia radicalization has been directed less against the Sunni than against the imperialist West and its supporters in the region, such as Saudi Arabia, Iraq (under Saddam Hussein), and Egypt (under Mubarak). Anti-Shia prejudice is widespread among the Sunni, manifested in massacres of Shia in Pakistan, Afghanistan, and in many other Muslim countries where they are in the minority. Jihadist radicalization thus takes on a sectarian dimension in the strict sense of the term, the Shia being considered inauthentic Muslims working secretly with the powers of evil to undermine Islam from within. Radicalized Shia appeal to the martyrdom of Husayn to legitimize their own struggle, death having become a fundamental element of their religiosity, so much so that, for the most radicalized, the wish to die seems to have replaced the desire to live. Among the Sunni, the symbolic dimension of radicalization is primarily marked by the desire to *cause* death, the death of the radical being only the ineluctable consequence of unfavorable power relations. No trace of dolorism is to be found in that type of martyrdom.

After the first year of the Islamic Revolution, Shia radicalization was orchestrated by the theocratic state under the aegis of the

41

charismatic Ayatollah Khomeini, primarily within Basij, an organization of young volunteers ready to sacrifice themselves to protect the Islamic Revolution in Iran. The Shia theocratic state has taken over all the mechanisms of radicalization and has repressed any form of expression that would seek to escape state domination. Basij, under the leadership of the Army of the Guardians of the Islamic Revolution (Pasdaran), is its official incarnation. Its members are trained to submit to death or to inflict it, under the army's supervision. The Lebanese Hezbollah, which was created by a branch of the Iranian Pasdaran, is also characterized by a strong organizational structure. There, radicalization comes about in opposition to the other Lebanese political groups but also to the Israeli army and, ever since the civil war in Syria, to opponents of Bashar al-Assad's regime. In that case, radicalization is linked to ethnicity: Shia versus Sunni in general, poor Shia versus rich Sunni and Maronite in particular, and Lebanese Shia versus Jewish Israeli. Mobilization also includes fundraising: Iran provides financial support to Shia radicality, particularly through emergency mutual aid networks (aid to victims of the Israeli offensive in July 2006, for example).

Shia radicalization is, on the whole, under the control of the Pasdaran in Iran via its Basij branch, and in Lebanon under that of the Hezbollah. In Iraq, however, it is primarily Muqtadā al-Sadr, leader of the Shia militia (the Mahdi army), who oversees ideologization and radicalization. That Shia cleric's bastion is Sadr City, a vast suburb in a northeastern district of the capital, Baghdad, where Iraqi Shia took refuge during their repression by Saddam Hussein in 1991. Muqtadā al-Sadr's partisans also seek to be the defenders of the "disinherited" (*mustadh'afun*), which gives their radicalization a social dimension that can be glimpsed in their politico-religious demands.

Unlike the Shia, radicalized Sunni no longer have a state to support them.[4] The process of radicalization comes about from below, on the foundation of tribal structures (in Yemen, in the geographic region of Waziristan in Pakistan, and in Libya, where, as in Afghanistan, warlords combine their private interests with the mobilization of militias).

In the early twenty-first century, Sunni radicalization was profoundly marked by the formation of the al-Qaeda network, based on the charisma of its leader Osama bin Laden and the devotion of its members, who consent to die in suicide attacks. Although the U.S. Army endeavored to dismantle the organization after the September 11 attacks and managed to eliminate some of its cadres in the 2000s, the group was able to regain its strength by adapting to the new situation through a strategy of decentralization and the constitution of small autonomous groups. These are joined to al-Qaeda by ideology and minimal communication, achieving an overall coherence in the ruthless struggle against the West, the United States in particular. The civil war in Syria and the Iraqi situation, where a Shia government is attempting to marginalize the Sunni, have given new impetus to jihadist groups that declare their allegiance to al-Qaeda or to groups in competition with it. The largest of these, the Islamic State of Iraq and al-Sham (ISIS), also called Daesh, has managed to constitute a new state between Syria and Iraq, encroaching on vast spans of territory in these two countries. ISIS has come into conflict with al-Nusra Front, a less rigorist jihadist group and a branch of al-Qaeda. Ayman al-Zawahiri, the head of al-Qaeda, has called for a division of the front between Iraq and Syria, whereas ISIS has sought to unify it under a single command. Nevertheless, the civil war in Syria, the deterioration of the situation in Iraq, and the opening of new jihadist fronts in sub-Saharan Africa have reinvigorated al-Qaeda, which still takes advantage of Pakistani tribal zones to harbor some of its cadres.

RADICALIZED WOMEN: A VERY SMALL MINORITY

Radicalization is a minority phenomenon, and that of women has been and remains even smaller in scope. Radicalized women can be found among the Chechens (the "Black Widows"), the Tamil Tigers (a third of the suicide attempts perpetrated by that separatist Marxist organization are said to have been carried out by women; see Pavey 2006), and Lebanese and Palestinian activists (André-Dessornes 2013), but also, in a few cases, within jihadism linked to al-Qaeda. Clearly, *shahida* (women martyrs) are not necessarily jihadists. In Lebanon, forty-one attacks were committed between 1982 and 1986 against the American, French, or Israeli military forces, according to Robert Pape; eight of them were the acts of radical Islamists, while the other thirty-three were carried out by Communists or Socialists, including six by women.

Between 1981 and 2011, according to the Chicago Project on Security and Terrorism (CPOST), of nearly 2,300 suicide attacks in the world, some 125 are said to have been committed by women, less than 5 percent of the total.

The first female suicide bombers were nationalists: the very first known, Sana'a Mehaidli, was for a year a member of the Syrian Nationalist Party, a secular organization. She blew herself up on April 9, 1985, killing two Israelis, to protest the occupation of South Lebanon by the Jewish state. In June 2000, two Chechen women detonated a truck loaded with explosives near a military base in Grozny, killing at least twenty-seven Russian soldiers.

On April 12, 2002, a female suicide bomber belonging to al-Aqsa Martyrs' Brigade, a secular and nationalist militant group, blew herself up in the Mahane Yehuda Market in Jerusalem, killing six people and injuring ninety. Subsequently, that group claimed responsibility for three other suicide attacks by women. It also created a women's struggle unit, Wafa Idris, named after the first female Palestinian suicide bomber, well before Hamas and the Islamic Jihad Movement had organized such a unit themselves. On October 4, 2003, Hanadi Jaratat, a twenty-six-year-old Palestinian woman, carried out a suicides attack for the Islamic Jihad at the Maxim restaurant in Haifa, killing twenty-one and injuring fifty-one.

In Amman on November 9, 2005, suicide bombers attacked three hotels. Among them was a woman, Sajida al-Rishawi, sister of Abu Musab al-Zarqawi's former right-hand man, killed by the Americans in Fallujah. Unlike her husband, also a member of the commando, she did not succeed in detonating her explosive belt. The attack killed fifty-seven and injured three hundred.[5]

In Turkish Kurdistan, women suicide bombers from the Kurdistan Workers' Party were involved in the struggle against the Turkish army in the 1980s.

Western converts to Islam can also be found among the female suicide bombers. For example, the Belgian Muriel Degauque, born in Charleroi in 1967, blew herself up in Baquba, Iraq, on November 9, 2005, killing five police officers and four civilians. At the age of thirty-five, Muriel had converted to Islam and taken the name Myriam. Through a member of al-Hidaya mosque in Brussels, she met a militant Salafist, a Belgian man whose mother was Moroccan. She married him and became radicalized, following the teachings of Sheikh Abu al-Shayma. In 2005 the couple went to Iraq. The husband was killed by the U.S. Army a few days after his wife's suicide attack, during another suicide bombing. Muriel and her husband belonged to a "suicide bomber network," whose founder, the Belgian-Tunisian Bilal Sughir, and two Belgian-Moroccan members received prison sentences.

Colleen LaRose, an American woman known as Jihad Jane, is said to have provided material support in 2009 for a terrorist plot to assassinate Lars Vilk, a Swedish author who caricatured the prophet Muhammad, giving him a dog's body. Another American woman, Jamie

Paulin Ramirez, was suspected of being the accomplice of an Algerian man, himself the prime suspect in the plot against Lars Vilk. After converting to Islam in 2009, she married a Muslim man she had met on the Internet and flew to Ireland, accompanied by her son by her first marriage, who had been renamed Wahid. Then there is the case of the British woman Samantha Louise Lewthwaite, known as the White Widow, whose husband blew himself up in the attack on the London Underground on July 7, 2005. She became associated with the Somali jihadist group al-Shabaab and may have taken part in terrorist activities.

For most female terrorists, the reason behind their involvement is the desire to avenge the death of a husband, brother, father, or other close member of the family. Women are the first to experience the ravages of war, the imprisonment of their men, the quasi-permanent state of siege (for example, in the Gaza Strip or Kashmir). In addition, men, in retaliation for having been the target of the occupation army or the forces of law and order, inflict profound humiliation on women. Organizations also have a strategic interest in women: they are less often suspected of being suicide bombers, and in many Muslim countries men are not allowed to frisk them. Finally, women sometimes have the desire to elevate themselves to the status of men by showing that they are capable of dying for a holy cause. They hope that if women can equal men in heroism in the face of death, it will become more difficult for men to deny women equality in life. Women's deaths as martyrs thus assume an antipatriarchal, even feminist dimension. That is why radical Islamist groups turn to female suicide bombers only under exceptional circumstances: they fear they will subsequently have to give up a number of prerogatives that their interpretation of the Quran and of the Hadith (the traditions or sayings of the Prophet) arrogates to men. The desperate situation of women in Muslim countries has been invoked to explain their involvement in suicide attacks, either because the enemy (American for the Iraqis and Afghans, Israeli for the Palestinians, Russian for the Chechens, and so on), in killing their husbands or members of their family, has exposed the women to such isolation that they cannot remake their lives (remarriage is very unlikely, even impossible) or because the women themselves have physical or psychological problems. Wafa Idris, the first Palestinian female suicide bomber, was infertile, and her husband's family forced her to divorce him; Muriel Degauque was born without a uterus. But these observations cannot be generalized to all women. The notion that they are forced to become suicide bombers also does not withstand analysis in most cases. There is a women's activism just as there is a men's activism, and a jihadist may very well be a woman; there is no need to impose more constraining norms on women than on men.

In the West, the radicalization of women in far-left secular movements came about through their active participation in attacks and in the very organization of terrorism. Such was the case for the Baader-Meinhof group (Red Army Faction), in which Ulrike Meinhof played a prominent role, as did Brigitte Asdonk, Monika Berberich, Irene Goergens, Petra Schelm, Ingrid Schubert, Rosemarie Keser, Brigitte Mohnhaupt, Suzanne Albrecht, Christine Dümlein, Monika Helbing, Birgit Hogefeld, and others. This was one of the first radical movements in which women participated almost on parity with the men, in both the planning and the execution of the attacks.

In the Muslim world, the radicalization of women follows a somewhat different path than that of men, given the importance of grievances associated with the death of a husband or loved one. That asymmetry has been less obvious in Europe, particularly within the Red Army Faction. In other respects, the radicalization of men and of women seems to result from the same factors: a sense of humiliation, deep resentment, an increased capacity to act through an organization or through ad hoc measures developed within a group, and finally, a desire to humiliate the humiliator. In cases of radical Islamism, it also entails earning the status of martyr and being rewarded with a privileged place in paradise; in the other cases, it means acquiring the aura of heroism and a place in collective memory.

3

The Jihadist Intelligentsia
and Its Globalization

Radicalization, then, entails a radical ideology and violent action, the combination of which gives rise to extreme forms of violence. The theories of the far left elaborated by the Frankfurt School (the denunciation of one-dimensional man by Herbert Marcuse), the Situationist International (Guy Debord's project to change the world by surpassing art through the upheaval of everyday life), or the group Socialisme ou Barbarie, founded by Cornelius Castoriadis and Claude Lefort, fostered and influenced the left wing in the 1970s, which gave rise to the terrorism of Action Directe in France. In addition, certain intellectuals (Jean-Marc Rouillan, Nathalie Ménigon, André Olivier, Régis Schleicher, and others) became personally involved in the group, combining action with theory to give an ideological meaning in situ to their violent acts. That duality of intellectuals—those who exerted an influence and those who were directly involved—was also found with the Red Brigades in Italy during the same period: intellectuals such as Antonio Negri, Mario Tronti, Romano Alquali, and Oreste Scalzone claimed an association with the leftist currents, while Alberto Franceschini, Renato Curcio, Enrico Fenzi, and others belonged to the group. So too in Germany, where the international leftist intelligentsia formed the ideological backdrop for the Red Army Faction and, within the revolutionary organization itself, intellectual-activists sought to elaborate a new theory of revolutionary action, even while participating in the extremist movement (that was the case, notably, for the authors of "Build Up the Red Army!" published in June 1970).

The same dual aspect of the intelligentsia can be found among the jihadists. Forming the backdrop is a jihadism dating at least to Sayyid Qutb and the Pakistani Abu A'la Maududi. Qutb was one of the first theorists to advocate waging permanent jihad until Islam takes root as a global religion that embodies the only politico-religious legitimacy. He was executed in 1966 by the Nasser regime in Egypt. Maududi was the theorist of *hakimiyya* (Islamic power). Their vision of an Islamic state was relayed by revolutionary Shia thinkers (in the 1970s Ali Shariati advocated "Red Shia," which combined the utopianism of a classless society with that of a society submitting only to Allah) and by dissident movements of the Muslim Brotherhood, such as Takfir wal-Hijra (Anathema and Exile). Founded in Egypt in 1971 by the engineer Shukri Mustafa, that movement emphasized the need for violent struggle, not only against non-Muslims but also against Muslims who refuse to wage jihad against the powers of evil (the West, but also all the Muslim states). Tanzim al-Jihad, founded in 1979 by Abd-al-Salam Faraj—an Egyptian engineer and the author of *Jihad, the Neglected Duty*—advocates the return to holy war against anti-Islamic forces (the new Crusaders and the Zionists). The assassin of Egyptian president Anwar Sadat was a member of that group.

The 1979 Islamic Revolution in Iran set in place a theocratic state conforming to the notions of Ayatollah Khomeini, resting on the principle of Governance of the Islamic Jurist, or Velayat Faqih. As a result, the struggle for a ruling power based fully on Islam no longer appears to be an inaccessible utopian dream.

The success of the Islamic Revolution in Iran reinforced radicalization. Some twenty years later, the attacks of September 11, 2001, filled radical Islamists with jubilation. These successes made the radicalized even more radical in their demands and shored up the conviction that, with divine assistance, the defeat of the "Crusader enemy" was possible. The Islamist dream of a global Islamic government (the neocalifate) is fueled by every partial success, which is seen as a step toward fulfillment of its aspirations.

Although heterogeneous, a large part of the Iranian intelligentsia, secular and religious, played a part in the 1979 Islamic Revolution in Iran: Shariati, Ayatollah Mahmoud Taleghani, Ayatollah Ruhollah Khomeini and his cleric disciples, Mehdi Bazargan (for a time), but also certain secularized, Marxist-leaning intellectuals, such as Jalal Al-e-Ahmad, who thought that an underdeveloped society such as Iran had to rely on a "revolutionary" Shia Islam to fight imperialism and the shah's autocratic power. In his lectures, Shariati also called for a revolutionary Shia movement, which would realize the dream of Marx and al-Mahdi (the twelfth hidden imam, the Shia messiah) by mobilizing the masses. What secular revolutions had been unable to achieve, revolution in the name of Islam would finally bring about. The major intellectuals were relayed by "minor intellectuals," who spread and amplified their message. Such was the case, notably, among the ranks of the clerical minority who supported Ayatollah Khomeini and among modernized young people who were invigorated by Shariati's ideas while attending his lectures at a new mosque, Hosseiniyeh Ershad, in a residential neighborhood of northern Tehran.

Modern radical Islamism began with the revolutionary tendencies that developed within the Muslim Brotherhood in Egypt (the Qutbist current, inspired by the ideas of Sayyid Qutb) and then found a new form in the revolutionary Shia movement of the 1970s–1980s, with Shariati and Ayatollah Khomeini. Later, it acquired a new field of application in its Sunni version, in Afghanistan under the ideological guidance of Abdullah Azzam, until the withdrawal of Russian troops in 1989 (Azzam was assassinated in Peshawar, Pakistan, in

November of that year). That movement found a new mobilizing theme—opposition to the West—under the leadership of bin Laden and Ayman al-Zawahiri, who served as organic intellectuals for the jihadist movement. At the same time, about ten radical Islamist "major intellectuals" worked to legitimize the extremist version of Islam, first in the Arab Sunni world, then, more broadly, in the West. The most eminent of these ideologues, including Abu Muhammad al-Maqdisi, Abu Basir al-Tartusi, Abu Mus'ab al-Suri, and Abu Qatada al-Filistini, exerted a decisive influence on jihadism in the Muslim world and beyond. They all agree on a few essential matters.

First, they call for a ruthless struggle against secular political systems that, inspired by the West, embrace the people's sovereignty. Any political philosophy based on the people is a form of idolatry (*shirk*); the cornerstone of any legitimate politics must be the sovereignty of Allah, and the people must submit to that transcendence. It is embodied in the Quran, the word of God, and in the Hadith, the traditions or sayings of the Prophet, collected by his companions and their students (the Salaf) in the first three centuries of Islam. Democracy is a particular target of radical Islamism, which sees it as a pernicious form of secularism whose ultimate aim is the destruction of Islam. Authoritarian governments in Muslim societies are also a form of idolatry (*taqut*) and, like democracies, they deny that Allah is the ultimate holder of political legitimacy. According to jihadism, autocracy and democracy are marked by secularism and an impious belief in the people as the ultimate source of legitimacy. Holy war must be waged vigorously against these heretical types of power, which are incompatible with Islam. Practically all the intellectuals mentioned have written a book or handbook characterizing democracy as idolatry and denouncing its perversity as a political system. In passing, they borrow a number of ideas from the Western far right and far left, cloaking them in Islamic terminology: for example, claims that the people are not the true holders of power but are supplanted in practice by the powers of money, the owners of capital, Zionists, Freemasons, and so on.

Second, they denounce Western imperialism, which enslaves the Muslim people of Bosnia, Afghanistan, Iraq, Palestine, and elsewhere. Islamic terminology (*istikbar* for imperialism, *istidh'af* for the exploited classes) is placed in the service of a vision that rejects Western domination while at the same time giving a theological content to anti-imperialism. That perspective attracts some Western young people, who no longer find in the far left the tools for battling imperialism and who see in that version of Islam the means to affirm their rejection of American hegemony, especially vis-à-vis the Palestinian question.

Third, they advocate a neopatriarchy to restore the sense of family by countering its modern disintegration, embodied in feminism, recognition of the equality of the sexes, and the legalization of homosexuality. Unlike Muslim reformism, fundamentalist Islamism and, even more, jihadism affirm the "complementarity" between men and women in the name of preserving the family. A man may marry as many as four women, while women have to submit to men in the realms prescribed by God. A woman's share of an inheritance is half that of a man's; her testimony in court has half the weight; her right to divorce is limited; and so on. That is an attractive view for men who have been thrown into confusion by feminism and who yearn for the stability of the patriarchal family.

The major jihadist intellectuals are echoed and amplified by many minor, homegrown intellectuals in Europe, who belong to the radical branches of Salafism. They learn Arabic in the hope of gaining access to the sacred texts and become vulgarizers of these philosophies, solidly rooted theologically in a specific interpretation of the Quran and the Hadith. Some Western intellectuals of the diaspora have a change in ideology and become the leading lights of jihadism. For example, Anwar al-Awlaki, an American imam of Yemeni descent, born in New Mexico in 1971, was an eminent member of al-Qaeda on the Arabian Peninsula and became its most influential ideologue. He was killed in Yemen by American drones on September 30, 2011. His jihadist sermons in English, broadcast over the Internet, influenced many believers and even inspired several attempted terrorist attacks in Great Britain and the United States, beginning in 2009. Awlaki was also an active contributor to the online magazine *Inspire*, in which practical advice on how to produce homemade bombs stands side by side with ideological texts justifying holy war against the United States and its allies. Several other Western jihadists contributed to that magazine: in particular, Adam Yahiye Gadahn, called Azzam the American; Samir Khan, a New Yorker who for a long time wrote a blog calling for jihad; and Yahya Ibrahim, a jihadist preacher who had lived in Canada.

The jihadist intelligentsia makes extensive use of globalization and the new forms of communication via the Web. Jihadists are becoming internationalized. They tap into the Muslim world but also seek converts and "born-again" Muslims. These individuals make radicalization much more dynamic, for they are familiar with Western culture and know how to act in a European or American environment without awakening suspicions, at least at the beginning of their involvement. Globalization also comes into play through a mingling of cultures and nationalities. The case of Anwar al-Awlaki and of some who collaborated with him is symptomatic. Born in the United States to Yemeni parents, Anwar al-Awlaki moved at the age of seven to Yemen, where his father became president of Sana'a University. After eleven years in that country, Anwar returned to the United States to attend Colorado State University and obtained a bachelor's degree in civil engineering, while serving as president of the Muslim Student Association. Combining a familiarity with Western culture and English and a knowledge of Arabic and jihadist ideologues (he was deeply influenced by Sayyid Qutb), he especially attracted young people from Anglo-American culture, which he understood much better than did the Arab jihadists. His ability to use the Web made "the Internet bin Laden" the ideal vulgarizer or intermediary intellectual, who simplified the theological views of the major ideologues of jihadism and served as something of a sounding board for Western young people. In 1993 he visited Afghanistan and was impressed by the writings of Abdullah Azzam, which provided a religious justification for jihad in Afghanistan: according to this view, jihad is an urgent obligation (*fardh al ayn*) when a Muslim country is occupied by non-Muslims. From 1996 to 2000, Awlaki served as imam at al-Ribat al-Islami mosque in San Diego, where two hundred to three hundred sympathizers followed his sermons. He was known and respected by some of the participants in the September 11 attacks.

Awlaki was one of the important figures in the radicalization of some Americans and Britons who subsequently committed murders or attacks in the United States or Great Britain—including Nidal Malik Hasan, responsible for the Fort Hood murders in Texas on November 5, 2009. He is also said to have inspired, or even recruited, the Nigerian Umar Farouk Abdulmutallab, who attempted to detonate plastic explosives on Northwest Airlines Flight 253 between Amsterdam and Detroit on December 25, 2009.

In 2002 Awlaki left the United States for Great Britain, where he spent several months. He gave lectures there in front of about two hundred young people, urging Western Muslims to never trust the heretics (*kuffar*, a pejorative term used by jihadists to refer to non-Muslims), because their goal was the eradication of Islam.[1] He lectured at various Muslim institutions in Great Britain, vaunting the merits of martyrdom and jihad and exhorting Muslims not to give themselves away. In 2004 Awlaki returned to Yemen. Imprisoned in 2006 under pressure from U.S. authorities for associating with al-Qaeda, he was released in December 2007 following intervention from his tribe. In March 2009, wanted by the Yemeni police, he went underground. In a video from March 2010, Awlaki directly accused the United States of attacking Muslims and urged American Muslims to revolt and, in the name of jihad, now an urgent duty, to do battle with it. According to the Western intelligence services, Awlaki was associated, directly or indirectly, with a dozen terrorist acts in the United States, Great Britain, and Canada. His exhortations influenced those who perpetrated the attacks in London in July 2005 and planned them in Toronto in 2006, as well as those involved in the attack on Fort Dix in 2007, among others. In all these cases, the people involved in the attacks had consulted Awlaki's messages and sermons on the Internet. He set up not only a website but also a Facebook page, which is consulted by many "fans" in the United States, most of them high school students.

That case, among many others, shows how new types of "global citizens" circulate easily among several countries and cultures by virtue of their multiculturalism and multiple nationalities and can exert a decisive influence on people who would otherwise be difficult to reach. Their sphere of influence further increases through use of the Web, especially Facebook and videos, in a "media jihad" that can become a powerful instrument in the radicalization of people on the other side of the world. Face-to-face contact is no longer necessary, just as possession of a shared culture loses its pertinence with globalization, whereas the hard-hitting, simplified message of oppression by the Western countries is always well received. Long-distance connections via the Internet with charismatic people, as well as the difficulty of uncovering such connections despite modern means of detection, make self-radicalization possible.

4

The Web

The Web exerts an influence as an instrument for organizing new forms of social action and for changing mental habits and ways of seeing and acting. The Arab Spring of 2010–2011 would not have assumed the form and intensity it did without the Internet, in particular Facebook and Twitter. The role of cell phones was just as decisive, especially when access to the Internet was cut off for a few days in Egypt, and Google facilitated the transfer of information to cell phones. In Iran as well, during the Green Movement in June–July 2009, the government's interruption of Internet service was in part offset by the use of cell phones.

But the Web is not just a "liberation technology," as has been said with some naïveté. It can just as well be an instrument that amplifies the capacity for violence in radical people or groups by allowing types of communication that forgo rigid structures and face-to-face meetings. In the government's hands, moreover, it can be a formidable instrument for conducting surveillance, even spying on citizens in their daily communications.

In short, the Web's role is not univocal or one-sided. In the case of radicalization, the Web not only plays a fundamental role in communications and exchanges among individuals; it is also an essential medium that can favor or even sustain radicalization among some people exposed to the material found there.

The Web opens a space that is neither private nor public in the traditional sense of the words. In this instance, it is a polarized space, that is, it aggregates those with elective affinities, who also set out to convince others to join them. It is a sectarian space, but it is not closed like a sect; it is public, but it does not have the openness of a real public space. Its virtuality consists not only of being unreal, but of dividing up the real following the rules of a multiple-value geometry, similar to Picasso's cubist paintings, which break and reorganize lines in accordance with reinvented vanishing points and points of convergence. In the quasi-public and semiprivate space of the Internet, one dimension assumes particular relevance: the counter-anomic, that is, the dimension that gives users the sense of participating in a "warm community," even if it is virtual. Many individuals in the West who suffer from anomie and the deterioration of social bonds find on the jihadist Web a particularly attractive community, inasmuch as it provides an intense sense of belonging, the sense that existence acquires meaning in the struggle against a perfidious enemy (the West), and above all that, in fighting the evil West, they will expel from their own souls the share of the devil that has found its way in. The jihadist Internet fulfills the function of an exorcist, comforting those who have no social bonds by inserting them into a redemptive community. These Internet users acquire a new identity, denouncing the devil's share within themselves: they are Westerners, low-status whites (*Petits Blancs*), tainted by evil and hence impure; or they are the children of immigrants, neither French nor Arab, embodying the evil of a dual "unbelonging," which they must expel from their being to recapture a "cleansed" identity, to become a Self in the struggle to the death against an external enemy but also an internal one, which made the constitution of a unified Ego impossible. The Web allows them to effect a change of identity in a half-oneiric, half-real universe teeming with thousands of texts, videos, films, and testimonials. Individuals can browse in a few hours what in the real world would take days or months. Space becomes condensed, time compressed, and identity narrows to a few redemptive aims: the fight to the death against the West, all-out war against an impure society, the desire to do battle with those who were formerly part of the familiar circle of "disidentity," of their old disaffiliation. The Web, bearing the incendiary message of jihadism, builds an identity, offers a vibrant community, eliminates anomie, and builds anew a world that is finally endowed with meaning and infinitely diversified in images and video footage that can be endlessly explored.

Radical Islamism gave rise to an intelligentsia that has revived jihadist themes while at the same time modernizing them, using the current political context to give them a meaning well beyond their purely theological or legal aspect. The new jihadist intellectuals have politicized Islam in a procedure undertaken first by Shia (with Shariati as the leading figure), then by Sunni (Maqdisi, Tartusi, Azzam, Suri, Abu Qatada). That new intelligentsia's entire oeuvre, almost all of it written in Arabic, was posted on the Web in the 1990s, and since the early twenty-first century has been translated almost in its entirety into English. Partial translations into French and other European languages are also available on a multitude of sites. Without the Internet, the jihadist literature—if only because of censorship—would certainly not have had the amplified influence it has had on almost every continent (with the probable exception of South America). Thousands of young people around the world have had free access to the Arabic version of the texts or to their many translations. Jihadist Internet forums have also allowed them to pursue subjects in greater depth and to meet other young people eager to become more involved in the struggle against an unjust world that oppresses Muslims, thus globalizing themes that in the past would have remained the prerogative of the more or less closed circle of intellectuals and the limited strata of educated people.[1] Sites showing battle scenes, executions, or techniques for producing homemade bombs allow young people without a purpose in life to become true masters of their own fate and that of others to experience on the Web a foretaste of what awaits them on the battlefield—a street, a café, a train station, or a plane they think they can blow up, or, even more vaguely, in Syria or Iraq, where they think they can fight for Islam against the heretical tyrant. The Web is "virtual" in this case less in the sense of being unreal than in the promise and enticements it contains of a reality to come, whose intoxicating pungency can be sampled in advance. It is the "reality" that Internet users make it their duty to realize after experiencing it in front of the computer screen. In performing their deadly task, they become Selves worthy in their own eyes. A perverse subjectivization, consisting of the promise of happiness and an irresistible desire to seek revenge on an unforgiving world, does away with anomie. Other people are now divided between heretical adversaries and devout friends, in a Manichaeism that puts an end to the anxiety of a meaningless universe.

A look at how post-9/11 jihadists were radicalized reveals the importance of the Web, either by virtue of the jihadist content of certain sites (individual self-radicalization) or by the exchange of views with other aspiring jihadists, which created connections culminating in joint plans for violent action in the name of radical Islam. In nearly all the cases considered, the Web played a significant role.

But the Web is not solely a means of propaganda in the hands of jihadists. It is sometimes used by antagonistic jihadist groups to settle scores. Twitter, for example, has played a fundamental role in the war waged between the two major jihadist groups in Syria, ISIS and al-Nusra Front, the official representative of al-Qaeda in Syria. In messages sent over Twitter, the two groups accuse each other of fomenting *fitna* (dissension among Muslims) and of weakening the Ummah vis-à-vis its sworn enemies, Assad's regime and the West of the Crusaders. Abu Khaled al-Suri, one of the leaders of the jihadist group Ahrar al-Sham (Free Men of the Levant) attacked ISIS on Twitter, accusing it of having initiated the fight against other jihadist groups in Syria. Al-Suri is also known to have been the representative of Zawahiri, leader of al-Qaeda in Syria.

Sometimes, within the same jihadist group, Twitter can be used to publicize internal dissensions that might otherwise go unnoticed. Between December 10, 2013, and January 21, 2014, for example, @wikibaghdady posted on the Web all the convoluted details of the lightning-fast advancement of Abu Bakr al-Baghdadi, emir of ISIS, and the expansion of that jihadist group from Iraq to Syria. His voice was silenced on January 21, 2014. And just as Twitter has become the most powerful instrument on the Web for propaganda and the recruitment of future members, it is also the means by which all the groups unveil the ploys and underhanded dealings of their adversaries, which contributes toward discrediting everyone in a ruthless propaganda war.[2]

European governments have become aware of the importance of the Web and the need to conduct surveillance and monitor the radical sites. Almost everywhere, a new criminal offense has been defined, even in democratic societies, one that could be called media jihad. In France, a law was enacted in December 2012, after the attacks by Mohamed Merah, authorizing the temporary detention of persons charged with "defending acts of terrorism" or inciting terrorism. Such was the case in particular for a twenty-six-year-old convert to Islam, Romain Letellier, who, under the pseudonym Abu Siyad al-Normandy, published many communiqués from the organization al-Qaeda in the Islamic Maghreb (AQIM). According to the public prosecutor's office, he is alleged to have played a significant role in translating into French and distributing issues 10 and 11 of the jihadist magazine *Inspire*. It is now possible, as the public prosecutor's office of Paris affirms, to speak of the "emergence of a virtual jihadist community, which attracts an increasingly broad and increasingly young audience, a vehicle for propaganda, radicalization, and recruitment, tipping the balance toward terrorism for isolated individuals."[3]

Romain Letellier, a convert to Islam at the age of twenty and married to a French Moroccan, is said to have acknowledged his active participation in the administration of the jihadist site Ansar al-Haqq, which distributes *Inspire*.[4] He was sentenced to a year in prison without possibility of early release by the criminal court of Paris.[5] In Great Britain, as in France, fomenting hatred in all its public forms is now subject to prosecution.

5

Financing Radicalization

Radicalization has a subjective and intersubjective dimension, but also an economic and financial one. Actions conducted without financial aid from certain groups or states are restricted to relatively low levels, whereas money allows extremists to acquire deadlier weapons and develop bigger, more violent operations. I shall confine myself to a discussion of the financing of jihadism, because of the scope of the movement, it being understood that the same type of problem arises in the various far-right and far-left groups, which are often financed by drug trafficking, hostage taking, and even piracy.

The role of charitable institutions in financing al-Qaeda and other jihadist groups, whether in the West or in Muslim countries, is well known. One of the tasks of the intelligence services has been to flush out this aid to extremists disguised as charitable fundraising, a task that the civil war in Syria has made even more complicated. Because Syria is run by an Alawite dictatorship, many Sunni, even if they do not belong to al-Qaeda or its ilk, feel religiously obligated to aid those struggling against the current regime, which is indiscriminately bombing and killing civilians, the overwhelming majority of them Sunni. In the war against the Assad regime, secularists are losing ground, and it is increasingly the radical Islamist fighters who are gaining the upper hand. Jihadist groups such as al-Nusra Front and a few others are thriving, with about ten thousand foreigners fighting alongside autochthonous members to overthrow the dissident Shia regime and replace it with a Sunni Islamic regime true to the jihadist vision of the neocalifate. Donors come forward in Saudi Arabia and in the United Arab Emirates: while assisting their Sunni brothers exposed to death and torture, they minimize the jihadist character of these groups and send their financial contribution to dubious charitable organizations, denounced as pro-jihadist by the United States. Two individuals from Qatar, for example, were accused by U.S. authorities of raising funds for the jihadist groups in Syria: Abd al-Rahman al-Nu'aymi, a university professor and former president of the Qatar Football Association, founding member of a large charitable group, and member of the Alkarama Foundation; and another member of that foundation, Abd al-Wahhab Muhammad Abd al-Rahman al-Humayqani, founder of the Rashad Union Party and promoter of the National Dialogue Conference, an organization that received financial assistance from the U.S. government. Nu'aymi claims that the accusation was made in retaliation for his criticism of U.S. policy in the region.

Certain associations, such as Madid Ahl al-Sham, which collects aid for Syria, have been cited by the Syrian jihadist groups as trustworthy, because some of the funds are directed to them.[1]

6

Sites of Radicalization

Despite globalization, the local aspect of radicalization retains all its pertinence, and geography is still an important factor, albeit reconfigured by the Web and transnational relationships. For a certain period of time, one country, region, city, neighborhood, or even one building or mosque will assume particular prominence as a center of radicalization. In the 1990s and early 2000s, the Finsbury Park Mosque in London was such a center of radical Islamism; Abu Hamza, one of the charismatic figures of jihadist Islam, preached there, and his sermons influenced an entire generation of young people, some of whom subsequently turned to violence in the name of holy war (see O'Neill and McGrory 2006). Likewise, the Dar al-Hijrah Islamic Center in Falls Church, Virginia, was one of the hot spots of radicalization in the United States during the 2000s. Anwar al-Awlaki was its imam from January 2001 to April 2002, and his charisma was able to attract young people to the radical version of Islam. Ahmed Omar Abu Ali, who also taught at that place of worship, was convicted in the United States in 2005 of providing material support to al-Qaeda.

Sometimes, neighborhoods show signs of radicalization when social and economic exclusion are combined with prejudice against the ethnic group and geographical origin of migrants or their descendants and with the preaching of radical Islam. In France, the city of Lyon and its *banlieues*, especially Vaulx-en-Velin and the neighborhood of Les Minguettes in Vénissieux, have been marked by recurrent Islamist radicalization. Khaled Kelkal, for example, who was responsible for the attack on the Saint-Michel metro station in Paris in July 1995, came from Vaulx-en-Velin. Likewise, of six French people imprisoned at Guantanamo Bay Naval Base, two were from Les Minguettes (Nizar Sassi and Mourad Benchellali). In the 1980s, the Lyon region was the starting point for the Beurs' March for civil rights (officially, the March for Equality and Against Racism; *Beur* is French slang for a child or grandchild of African immigrants), and the failure of that movement played a role in the radicalization of the area, as did the strategic situation of Lyon as a hub connecting Paris, Switzerland, and Marseille. Radical Islamism took root in the large Algerian community of the region at the onset of the Algerian crisis that followed the army's coup d'état in 1992, in large part because the Beurs' March had failed.

Lille and surrounding cities, especially Roubaix, were also sites for the development of jihadism in France, particularly with the "Roubaix gang," whose members committed multiple violent armed robberies in the Nord-Pas-de-Calais region in 1996 and perpetrated a car-bomb attack during the G7 summit in Lille in late March 1996. The gang, which combined radical Islamism and organized crime, was run by two Frenchmen who had converted to Islam: the presumed leader Christophe Caze, a fifth-year medical student; and Lionel Dumont, who came from a large family and was passionate about performing humanitarian acts. The members had become acquainted at the mosque on rue Archimède in Roubaix, where they established ties with Muslims who had fought in Bosnia in 1994–1995. The Algerian Islamist Abdelkader Mokhtari, nicknamed Abu el-Maali, played a significant role in getting them involved in jihadism.[1] In the Roubaix gang, converts for the first time appeared unequivocally among the jihadists.

In Great Britain, southeast London—Brixton in particular—has seen the emergence of radical Islamists since the 1990s; in most cases, they were recruited from the West Indian (Afro-Caribbean) communities, though the majority of that population is Christian.[2] In that geographically circumscribed space, the Islam of converts has a new function: it is "the religion of the oppressed," of those who suffer racial discrimination and segregation, under a white power that has mangled the message of equality and dignity. The embrace of Islam in that case allows converts to reverse the roles. Whites are heretics and become the pole of evil, and black believers occupy the pole of good.

The sites of radicalization have tended to change over time, if only because of increased vigilance on the part of the police. In France in the 1990s and early 2000s, radicalization occurred in mosques (or in apartments used as places of worship), sometimes without the knowledge of the leadership: Farid Benyettou preached to young disciples in a relatively private setting at Addawa Mosque in Paris. It must now occur elsewhere, because the intelligence services conduct increasingly close surveillance on places of worship, and the mosque leadership exercises greater control. Currently, it is on the Internet, in groups of friends living near one another, in prison (see chapter 8 below), or even within philanthropic associations and during travel abroad (especially to Pakistan, Yemen, and Egypt) that young people attempt to become affiliated with a group or to constitute one.

Until the early 2000s, London ("Londonistan" to Islamists) was the destination of choice for individuals who were already radicalized or were searching for an affiliation with a jihadist network. Radical Maghrebi Islamists who were wanted by the police in France or

North Africa took up residence there as a means of escape. That channel has now largely dried up, particularly under American pressure after the attacks of September 11, 2001, and British surveillance after those in London in July 2005. Jihadists in both Great Britain and France, in their attempts to organize, opt less and less frequently for the mosque and increasingly for the Web for bonds of friendship.

7

The Ambiguous Role of Frustration in Radicalization

There is no direct causal relationship between frustration and radicalization. Although frustration does not lead automatically to radicalization, it can, however, exert a greater or lesser influence on certain types of individuals, especially the psychologically fragile. The growing complexity of forms of sociability and the anomie of modern society, as well as social and economic disparities, prompt in these individuals the feeling that humanity is divided between those who are well-to-do and integrated and those trapped in a state of precariousness that threatens to collapse into poverty, even destitution. At the same time, so-called social media decompartmentalize different parts of the world, often in a very complex way. The Internet and virtualized social relations can also contribute to mental and social disconnection, modes of being that can result in deviant behavior. These weaknesses can be exploited by leaders who take advantage of psychologically fragile outcasts. Many statistical studies show that, in Europe, the great majority of the radicalized (especially jihadists) are recruited from among outcasts (Sageman 2008; Leiken and Brooke 2006). Paranoid tendencies may give rise to an exaggerated interpretation of the reality of insufficient resources, racism, and ghettoization, which leads fragile individuals to attribute such deficiencies and dysfunction to a deliberate will to destroy the particular group to which they belong (Muslims, "native stock" French people, Jews, blacks). Loners or "virtualized" individuals, pathologically magnifying the facts behind their frustration, hold these conditions entirely responsible for their own abject poverty and that of their group. Then, often in the name of an imagined community of which they believe themselves to be the spokespersons, they seek to exact their revenge and make society as a whole pay. Social struggle gives way to infrasocial forms of antagonism based on identity.

Accumulated frustrations, especially when they are related to Islam, can spur the radicalization of individuals who at first do not necessarily know very much about that religion. Islamist radicalization does not require extensive knowledge of the religion of Allah. Most of the time, it is *after* radicalization that believers are overcome by the desire to learn more about Islam in its jihadist version. In France, that phenomenon is apparent both in the *banlieues* and in prison. The children and grandchildren of Maghrebi immigrants are profoundly "de-Islamized" before their conversion to radical Islamism. As I observed in the field,[1] it is not a deep preexisting knowledge of the religion that leads to radicalization in the *banlieues*; on the contrary, it is a profound *lack* of education, an exaggerated credulity, a form of naïveté resulting from misunderstanding or ignorance of Islam, that favors extremism.

The hatred of society borne by young people from the ghettos is transposed all the more easily to religiosity in that they are unversed in Islam and readily identify jihad with anti-imperialist struggle, *taqut* ("idolatry") with secular political regimes, or *jahiliyya* ("ignorance") with democracy or any political system that is not the Islamic theocracy they hope and pray for, without necessarily knowing all that theocracy would entail. More generally, frustrations that for the most part are not of a religious nature are apt to be converted into a religious repertoire that can give them a sacred meaning, pushing some people toward jihad as a form of revolt. The wars in Afghanistan,

Iraq, and other Muslim countries (the French army's involvement in Mali, for example) have created the feeling among these young people that Islam is under assault by Christian or atheistic powers and that its defense is an urgent religious duty (*fardh al ayn*). That sense of allegiance to a sometimes very remote Islamic world also indicates how fragile national feeling can be for this generation, which finds it difficult to bear segregation in the *banlieues* or poor neighborhoods, financial insecurity, and rejection by society. That rejection is amplified in the imagination and attributed to a systematic willfulness and anti-Islamic intentions that have little basis in reality.

8

The European Model of Radicalization

Although radicalization is taking ever more diverse forms, its expression in environmental, anti-abortion, or animal-rights activism is unusual in Europe. The dominant schemas are still political Islamism and the far right (radicalized skinheads, various groups opposing Muslim European identity, lone wolves like Anders Breivik).

There is an optimal age, between about fifteen and forty, for those who embrace violent action based on an extremist ideology. After that age, some (for example, a portion of those radicalized in the 1990s who played a leading role in the attack on the Saint-Michel metro station in Paris in 1995) more or less settle down and declare that they want to return to a normal life or put an end to violent acts, which they judge increasingly unrealistic, though they do not necessarily abandon their extremist ideology. Others continue to embrace violent action. One often senses a fear on their part of losing their "class standing": after several years in prison and isolation, they are well aware that they no longer have a place within the new terrorist constellations and that, though still respected, they are marginalized because of their age. The few leftists and especially jihadists approaching fifty do not age well: for the most part, they persist in remaining in their ideological straitjackets and nurse the ideal of violent action, sustained by an ideology that remains as radical as ever. At least in Europe, those who have done prison time—I was able to meet a dozen of them—are in denial about the aging process and display an ideological stability. For them, it would be tragic to admit their failure to champion the proletarian revolution (for the far left) or the neocalifate (for jihadists).

Those under forty adopt a hard line: they intend to "avenge themselves" on an unjust society and have an unshakable conviction in the need for violent action against a country or state complicit with the anti-Islamic forces. Generational differences observable outside prison are found in nearly identical form on the inside: the most formidable supporters of radicalization are not the grandfathers or fathers but the sons, especially after intelligence services have identified radical tendencies in their elders. Among the younger generations in Europe, jihadists are for the most part (but not entirely) young people whose life course has been chaotic (delinquency, then the adoption of an ideological hard line) and who seek an identity in radical action that they have been unable to find elsewhere. Jihadism is an act of "identity recovery," self-unification, in a society where identity is multiple (its positive dimension) but also shattered (its negative dimension). Especially for young people who live in the ghetto, jihadism is clearly attractive for its antisocial aspect (hatred of society is transcribed onto a sacred register) and its antidomination dimension: they resent social domination, but instead of adopting a philosophy of action that challenges it constructively over time, they opt for the short-term radical solution of doing battle with a social or political order that consequently becomes "heretical," "godless," and "diabolical." All the same, jihadism cannot be reduced to negativity. Its "positive" dimension lies in an individual's self-promotion as someone with an identity that is unified (even ossified, given the extreme coherence of a vision that excludes and anathematizes everything in opposition to its aims) within a heroic self-perception. Such individuals become heroes by espousing the logic of martyrdom and jihad in its extremist version and making media coverage a fundamental element of their identity. They assert themselves as people who count. They take pride in instilling fear when they had previously inspired arrogant contempt or rejection on the part of "whites," that is, those who have been successful, including middle-class Arabs. Radical Islamization occurs from within—it is the result of an extremely precarious psychological state and social anomie—but also from without, in accordance with globalized mechanisms that often extend beyond the national context. Events as they unfold beyond the borders find relays for transmission to potential jihadists via the Internet, but also through charismatic personalities or more or less secret organizations.

LOW-STATUS WHITES

Low-status whites—those Patricot (2013) calls *les Petits Blancs*—or "white trash," as one young criminal from an immigrant background put it, are those at the bottom of the social ladder who feel that their economic and social poverty has gone unrecognized and believe themselves subject to contempt twice over: silent contempt on the part of "real whites," that is, those who are economically and socially integrated, but also aggressiveness combined with rejection (creating the sense that they no longer belong) on the part of young people from the *banlieues*, who have very ambivalent feelings about the low-status whites who live in the same neighborhood they do.

Low-status whites are distrustful of "Arabs," who in their view monopolize the attention of the public authorities and, through noisy rebellion, overshadow the silent indignity in which they themselves feel trapped. They feel silently "racialized" by republican elites and by a population that looks askance at them or, even worse, does not see them at all, for in some people's minds poverty is the exclusive lot of the *banlieues* and immigrants. That contempt on the part of society, stemming from disregard or ignorance, gives low-status whites the impression that, strictly speaking, they do not exist. The vast majority lead their lives with grim resignation, in the anonymity of poverty and daily economic difficulties, without making a fuss or staging a public revolt. They accept their lot as if it were preordained, are outraged in their heart of hearts, but generally do not let it show, even in political ways. Some do subscribe to the Front National (FN), which has replaced the Communist Party as the defender of the little people. The FN enhances the self-image of low-status whites, restoring their confidence in their lives and offering them a future in which they would recover their dignity in a France finally recaptured by the French. Another portion of them, limited all in all, turn to violent extremist organizations or to radical Islamist groups, converting to the religion of Allah. Their attitude, then, can range from the solitude of mute suffering to cries of rage in the Front National or the embrace of jihadism. In the latter two cases, revenge seems possible. The Front National gives low-status whites the capacity to reclaim their place in a new France rid of undesirable foreigners, whereas jihadism offers them the opportunity to avenge themselves on the white people who have always held them in contempt.

Only a minority of low-status whites become radicalized. My analysis focuses on these groups and on their mental states and subjectivity, key elements in their radicalization. To a large degree, the symbolic triangular relationship among whites, low-status whites, and Arabs (represented as inassimilable foreigners) is the key to the radicalization of low-status whites in the direction of extremist violence, whether secular (far right) or religious (Islamist).

For young Arabs, "white trash" are the countermodel of real white people, whom they hate and envy. Being less than zero, often even lower than the Arabs in their social and economic degradation, these impoverished whites belie the white-people stereotype. They are less economically secure, often lacking even the resources Arabs have in the neighborhood, namely, group solidarity, an informal mutual aid system, and, for some *gris* (literally, "grays," young people from immigrant backgrounds living in "bad neighborhoods"), a capacity for extralegal activities that bring in extra money and social consideration, at least on the few blocks they call home. Those whom some call *caillera* (French back slang for *racaille*, "scum") manage to make ends meet through gang solidarity and a thorough knowledge of the relatively complex forms of criminality in the neighborhood. Low-status whites, for their part, are helpless, not enjoying the advantages of solidarity, which they may seek in skinhead-type groups or among the Arabs. Some of them, living alone on the fringes of big cities, end up homeless, misunderstood by others and rejected by their families or former associates. Low-status whites blur the idealized image of white people, whom young ghettoized Arabs have learned to hate for their arrogance, self-importance, and easy conscience, even while envying them for their supposedly rich lives. Inferior rather than superior, feeling worthless rather than like full-fledged citizens, they are impossible to envy and make hatred of white people pointless. That is why they inspire not sympathy but contempt combined with resentment. Far from showing compassion toward them because of their inferior status, Arabs often begrudge them even their failure to live up to the image of the white people they hate.

Low-status whites, for their part, do not feel at home in the neighborhoods where they live. They feel rejected and despised on two fronts. Often living in areas where young people from immigrant backgrounds, criminals or Islamists or both at once, taunt them by their mere presence and their *banlieue* culture, low-status whites may be tempted by extremism—on the right, to do battle with Arabs, or in its radical Islamist form, to combat whites. If they are too discouraged to act, they withdraw into themselves, confining themselves within a life of loneliness and a sense of worthlessness, which gradually make them unable to take responsibility for themselves. Their existence is increasingly marginal, and they may abandon themselves to a nagging anxiety. The ensuing racism is the consequence of their malaise in a world where they have no place, a reaction to the aggressiveness of young Arabs, who, they believe, are assisted and supported by the state through programs that provide aid to large families, unemployment benefits, and so on. Meanwhile, they themselves are ignored, reduced to an inferiority imposed on them as the indirect effect of social measures that, in their view, work to their disadvantage. The social image that low-status whites have of themselves, of Arabs, and of integrated whites is painful to them. There is a repressed hatred in low-status whites, whether they live in the *banlieue* or in prison. No longer feeling at home, they call for a return to the former state of affairs, which would exclude the Arab and restore to them a dignity of which they have been robbed by all sides. But who is denying them their dignity? Immigrants and their descendants, to be sure, but also "regular" whites, who despise them and crush them with a sometimes pitying contempt, often concealed behind indifference or, quite simply, behind ignorance of their very existence. For "regular" whites, low-status whites do not exist or exist only as trash. They are bums and beggars who eat at soup kitchens, disturbed people to be avoided or grudgingly helped but kept at a distance. As a result, low-status whites become radicalized partly to exact their revenge. They may do so by subscribing to far-right groups that "kick Arab butt," finding there a justification for their ferocious hatred of immigrants, who they think are culturally inferior but socially superior because of their networks of sociability, the assistance they receive from the government, and the proceeds of their criminal activity. Racism among low-status whites is experienced as alienation. As one young man, imprisoned for aggravated assault in a northern metropolis, put it, "Got together with buddies to beat up Arabs we came across in the alleys near the train station, when they were by themselves or out with girls. We got back at them." "Why Arabs?" "They're taking away our jobs, our girls, our social benefits, plus they rub it in our faces, they hate us and want to impose their religion on us and their way of life and of looking at things. Sometimes they come in groups to make war on us."

Young Arabs, for their part, develop reverse racism, which is used as a justification for their delinquency and their violent actions against society. In interviews conducted in prison, they often mention the discrimination they suffer because of their origins, their accent, or their life in bad neighborhoods. This reverse racism is caused by a society that marginalizes, excludes, and denies dignity to them. They are treated like second-class citizens in a "neither/nor" that strips away their identity: neither French (in France) nor Arab (in North Africa), they are "dirty Arabs" in France and "dirty French" in their parents' homelands.

As for low-status whites, their racism is brought on by their social situation, not by a radical hatred of Arabs or others. Made to feel inferior on two fronts, through symbolic racism they restore a self-image that has been seriously damaged by the erosion of their identity. They suffer a different form of neither/nor: neither "French from good families" (middle-class whites) able to lead normal lives as citizens, nor Arabs able to benefit from social assistance. They are beaten down from both sides, somewhat like the Arabs they hate but with whom they share a certain social and economic exclusion. They, however, give it a different emotional tone: they no longer feel at home, as if they were in internal exile, inexorably marginalized, their demands disregarded by politicians on the left and right alike. They exact their revenge on two distinct, even antagonistic, fronts: they may join far-right groups and flaunt their membership (they are no longer alone and abandoned), with the aim of fighting Arabs, but they may just as readily convert to Islam and make common cause against "regular" whites. In that case, the trajectory of their radicalization coincides with that of young Muslims from immigrant backgrounds, though it is distinguished from it by the choice initially offered them. But low-status whites, in their hatred of Arabs, and more generally Muslims, may become radicalized as well in a third, original sense: even while maintaining their "European" identity and subscribing to far-right views, they may kill whites to "wake them up" to the looming threat of Muslims, as the Norwegian Anders Breivik did.

Although many are financially insecure, some low-status whites belong to the middle classes and may adopt a reflexive radicalization through imaginary constructs. It is well known that the Front National vote, especially in certain departments of northeastern France, in small towns, and in rural areas, is associated not with a large presence of Arabs but with the kind of fear they inspire, which those afraid of losing their social standing or identity transpose to their imaginary world. Their imaginary under assault, extremist rightists have a sense of victimhood (Europe, they believe, is the victim of the Muslims), and their sense of reality is focused on "the Islamic enemy," who must be combated at all cost to preserve their own European identity (Norwegian in Breivik's case). Violence thereby becomes legitimate. That belief distinguishes such an identity from that of the Front National's electoral base, which does not publicly advocate physical violence. Modern life makes that change of register to the imaginary possible: white people can take on the identity of low-status whites by means of self-radicalization, that is, through the use of the Internet and auto-indoctrination, without having to endure the socioeconomic conditions of low-status whites. In the past, bourgeois intellectuals could become supporters of the proletariat out of sympathy, but underlying that support was a rational view of things. It is now possible to transport oneself to the other's world in one's imagination, to remain and settle in, without actually being there. Low-status whites, real or imagined, may harm or kill other whites to sound the alarm and prevent the catastrophe they see, in an apocalyptic vision of the world in which Europe loses its identity and submits to Islam.

Both forms of radicalization, right-wing extremism and jihadism, allow low-status whites to reintegrate themselves: the anomie of their precarious condition is combated by their membership in a group that rescues them from isolation and, above all, restores their dignity. Most often, however, they sink into mute despair, raging inside without finding a release valve.

RADICAL ISLAMISTS

A combination of two factors pushes people toward radicalization: living conditions in the ghetto (Lapeyronnie 2008), that is, the French *banlieues* or the poor districts of Great Britain, and a feeling of intense dehumanization, which convinces them that the situation is hopeless, that all doors are closed to them and that their horizons are definitively blocked. That feeling is a subjective intensification of the cruel reality of social prejudices and racism, which are relatively diffuse and less radically exclusive than the "victimized" claim. After all, many French of North African descent lead successful lives in France, join the middle classes, and break out of the vicious cycle of poverty, criminality, and imprisonment. Nevertheless, looming in the background of radicalized subjectivity in Europe, particularly in France, is the fantasy of imprisonment in a closed and dehumanized world with no hope of escape. So long as that feeling is not connected to an ideology, it is expressed either as criminality (a way for subjects to extricate themselves by flouting the laws of a society that denies them dignity and by adopting the consumerism of the middle classes) or as a dark despair, often expressed as overaggressiveness. In the latter case, the slightest look from whites can lead to totally disproportionate violence from *gris*, and anyone wearing a uniform—a police officer, a gendarme, a ticket inspector on public transport, even a firefighter—is considered an enemy by virtue of being an agent of the state or a symbol of social success and an orderly life. That combination of despair, bitterness, and resentment is called hatred by young people and rage by sociologists (Dubet 2008 [1987]).

It is when that hatred finds an ideological foundation and comes to be considered holy that it goes beyond mere aggressiveness and delinquency and becomes radicalized. Now subjects no longer seek to extricate themselves individually but rather to save Islam and the Muslims, for whom they become self-proclaimed spokespersons, fighting head-on an "ungodly" and "idolatrous" world as knights of faith. That transposition of rage to the religious domain occurs all the more easily in Europe, where the young poor are ignorant of Islam. Their lack of understanding opens the door to a facile identification with the religion of Allah, solely on the register of jihad. The violent version of religiosity legitimizes the war against a social order in which subjects have never felt like other people, have always been treated as inferior, "like bugs," as a young man from the *banlieue* said, rejected on all sides and in turn rejecting everyone, in an aggressiveness that has become an integral part of their identity.

A few examples may serve to illustrate that state of affairs. In the West Indian communities of Great Britain, individuals but also sometimes groups of young people convert to Islam and subscribe to a bellicose version of it. Such was the case for Abdullah al-Faisal (known as Faisal al-Jamaikee, Faisal the Jamaican), who converted to Islam and proclaimed himself a preacher. In his sermons, he quoted verses from the Quran but also the words of Marcus Garvey, the Jamaican leader who denounced the hegemony of whites and advocated the return of blacks to Africa. Abdullah al-Faisal attempted to mobilize blacks in the name of Islamic justice against the iniquity of whites, that is, non-Muslims who oppress Muslims and blacks. In some of his sermons, he called for the murder of non-Muslims, earning himself a prison sentence in 2003 (as-Salafi and al-Ashanti 2011; Baker 2011). For al-Faisal, Islam is the authority that makes it possible to denounce injustice toward blacks, the hegemony of white

82

people being unjustified. Islam is the religion of the oppressed, who can break the vicious cycle of oppression only by declaring war against the ungodly whites.

The case of Zacarias Moussaoui is also symptomatic in its way. Born in France to Moroccan parents in 1968, he lived with his mother after his parents' divorce. She attempted to raise four children "in the French manner," isolated from their Moroccan and Islamic roots, if only to accelerate their integration. Zacarias drank alcohol, dated an Algerian girl of French descent without marrying her, had Jewish friends, and at times did not hesitate to smoke hashish. He knew nothing about Islam. After graduating from high school, he managed to earn a vocational training certificate in sales and marketing in 1990. In the early 1990s, he began to develop a warped sense of identity and undertook a search for his roots in Islam. He attended the Montpellier mosque, then in 1992 left for London to improve his English, after obtaining an associate degree in business administration from the Université Paul-Valéry Montpellier. At that time, London—"Londonistan"—was one of the bases where Islamists could establish connections and form plans, taking advantage of the British government's tolerance. Moussaoui was influenced by the sermons of Abu Hamza, the imam of Finsbury Park Mosque, and by those of Abu Qatada. He established ties, both emotional and material, with radical Islamists (they aided him financially) in a geopolitical context where the troubles assailing the Muslim world in Bosnia, Palestine, Algeria (where civil war was raging), and elsewhere were attributed to the West, particularly the United States. He traveled to Afghanistan, where he made the acquaintance of Khalid Sheikh Mohammed, the mastermind behind the September 11 attacks, but his erratic behavior made others wary, and he was marginalized. His trip to the United States in February 2001, where, financed by Islamic extremists, he signed up for flying lessons, aroused the suspicions of the authorities. He was incarcerated on August 16 of the same year, before the attacks on the Twin Towers, and was sentenced to life in prison in May 2006. For Moussaoui, Islam, the antidote to his identity crisis, could take root only as open warfare against the West, land of godlessness and domination.

Mohamed Merah, the "scooter killer," acted more than a decade after Moussaoui but with a similar ideological vision. In March 2012, he killed seven and wounded six others in Toulouse and Montauban. Three Jewish children were among his victims.

A glimpse of the anthropology of his family makes intelligible (without explaining it irrefutably or allowing one to draw up a profile) his inclination to sever his ties with society and his absence of moral conscience vis-à-vis his victims, especially the three Jewish children he killed in cold blood. Merah, like Moussaoui, came from an immigrant family, and his mother too found herself raising her children on her own. His father had a fanatical, if not radical, view of religion, as did his mother, his maternal uncle Hamid, and a Franco-Syrian mentor who supposedly played the role of ideologue. This man was implicated by Abdelghani Merah, Mohamed's brother, in a book written in collaboration with a journalist (Merah and Sifaoui 2012). In addition, the other brother, Abdelkader, and one of his two sisters, Souad, were Islamists. In that family of two sisters and three brothers, criminality was pervasive: the father was imprisoned in France for trafficking in marijuana; the elder brother, Abdelghani, served a short prison term; the younger one, Abdelkader, was detained for assault and drug trafficking while still a minor, then went to prison for assaulting his elder brother, who was married to a Jewish woman. Abdelkader attended Salafist religious schools in Cairo, where in 2010 he studied the Quran with his sister Souad. She was prosecuted by the Egyptian courts for perjury. Her first husband was a drug trafficker, her second a Salafist, and she was designated by the French intelligence services as a "follower of radical Islam."[1] Souad went to Egypt in 2010 to study Islam and learn Arabic, the language

84

of the Quran. She professed a view of Islam in which violent action on the part of other believers seemed legitimate, though she herself did not resort to it (in an interview with her brother Abdelghani, filmed without her knowledge, she declared she was proud of Mohamed's actions). Her sister Aïcha and her brother Abdelghani did not subscribe to radical Islam and felt estranged from their two brothers and elder sister. Mohamed Merah, the youngest in the family, was born into a broken family where a climate of domestic violence and religious intolerance reigned. He was often left alone by his mother and, at the age of six, was placed in a foster family, then transferred to a group home. Unstable, sad, subject to violent outbursts, he failed at school. He was often scolded and physically abused by his brother Abdelkader. He himself sometimes attacked those who interfered with the satisfaction of his desires: in 2002 he struck a social worker in the face because he could not spend the weekend with his family. He assaulted girls, was abusive to teachers, stole, spewed insults. Even his mother complained of his violence. He committed multiple illegal acts, accumulating fourteen convictions while still a minor. Mohamed belonged to a gang that in 2007 organized a "homejacking," breaking into a house and taking possession of a 4x4. He escaped the police driving 110 miles an hour, but not before crashing into the vehicle belonging to the gendarmerie, injuring a noncommissioned officer and a volunteer in the reserves.[2] He was proud because the footage of the pursuit was shown on television. In Mohamed Merah's case, violence had three dimensions: the real, the symbolic, and the ecstatic. He experienced the real dimension in relation to others, inflicting injury or death on them without the slightest regret, because of his dual allegiance to jihadism and crime. In fact, the two allegiances justified and reinforced each other. He lived the symbolic aspect in his imagination, playing violent video games or repeatedly watching movies, such as the revenge-themed *Faster* from 2010 or films of war and destruction, which fascinated him.

Finally, the ecstatic dimension intoxicated him, making him forget the fear of death and erasing any pangs of conscience. His adherence to radical Islam, which glorifies martyrdom as the guarantee of an eternal life of happiness, made him heedless of the risk of dying. He attributed to God the fact that he had escaped the law in the 4x4 chase. To him, his activities were sacred. But they were also adventures in which his Ego was sublimated in transports of joy. He became a negative hero, tapping into a subculture of violence where brutality is "natural" and the social contract of peaceful coexistence null and void. The ecstatic dimension was reinforced narcissistically by video footage. Whenever he committed a crime, Merah wore a GoPro camera around his neck: his films were intended for the global audience of Al Jazeera, though the channel refused to broadcast them. Images were an intrinsic part not only of his crime but also of his identity: he put himself in the shoes of the "mujahedeen" and killed, supposedly, to save Islam. Images glorify the negative hero, who gains in self-esteem in direct proportion to the hatred he inspires in society.

Merah visited many countries, including Pakistan, Egypt, Syria, Lebanon, Jordan, Tajikistan, and Afghanistan. He attempted to make contact with al-Qaeda and sent 186 text messages to numerous foreign countries between September 2010 and February 2011.[3] His somewhat rudimentary knowledge of Arabic and the distrust on the part of the organizations with which he tried to associate himself are said to have impelled him to act alone, at least in the murders he committed. Groups such as Forsane Alizza (Knights of Pride), which advocates the worldwide enforcement of Sharia, certainly influenced him, but he perpetrated his crimes on his own.

Merah, Moussaoui, and several others all had in common disrupted family lives, an accumulation of grievances real and imaginary against society, the desire to do battle with it by turning to a life of crime, and a profound sense of social injustice combined with an effaced identity (neither French nor Arab). Jihadist radicalization seemed to them a way to overcome indignity and to set down roots in the sacred. The result was an absolute legitimization of violence against others, based on victimhood: "I am an absolute victim of a society that has totally excluded me, so I am justified in being wholly immoral toward it."

THE VICTIMIZED YOUNG

In Europe, particularly in France, the large presence of Muslims is linked to efforts to industrialize the Old Continent that began in the early 1960s. The need for unskilled labor to ensure the economic development of countries ravaged by two world wars propelled the authorities to encourage immigration. Naturally, to find the necessary labor force, the various European countries turned to their colonies or former colonies, to the countries nearest at hand, or to those with which they had cultural ties: North Africa for France, India and Pakistan for Great Britain, Turkey for Germany. As it happened, a large percentage of that labor force belonged to the Muslim religion. After three generations, a large portion of the children and grandchildren of these unskilled laborers, though they possess the nationality of their elders' host country, live under conditions of great poverty and even social exclusion. Although some have managed to join the middle classes and become economically integrated, many remain poverty-stricken and their full citizenship is denied them, as suggested by the nicknames "Paki" in English and *Arabe* or the racial slur *bougnoule* in French. This denigration is by and large a male phenomenon; girls in France, provided they do not wear the hijab, are much more easily accepted than boys. Discrimination results in a much higher unemployment rate among these populations than within society at large and their concentration in neighborhoods with bad reputations, where social segregation is acute and the standard of living much lower than the national average, where criminality is more prevalent and the educational level lower.

The lives of these young people, who spend the greater part of their time loitering in front of their apartment buildings, were designated by a popular expression in the 1980s: *la galère*, "the gallery." The young unemployed drift into criminality, in a state of mind considered characteristic of the end of industrial society and the collapse of social institutions (Dubet 2008 [1987]). In Great Britain, the expression "street life" seems to correspond to that reality: the young who adopt that lifestyle combine delinquency, a lack of social perspective, physical violence, and the conviction that the middle classes (whites, or, more precisely, the socially and economically integrated) enjoy a status inaccessible to them.

Some young people in these neighborhoods live as if they have no future, as if the hope of economic integration into the larger society is a delusion. That state of mind, which I will call *victimhood*, rests on a profoundly pessimistic view of social existence by the excluded strata, combined, in the case of young people from immigrant backgrounds, with a rejection of their "Arab" identity. Some of these young people who do not practice the religion nevertheless identify with it, in an attempt to overcome symbolically a double denial—of their Arabness and their Frenchness (or in Britain, their Pakistani identity and their Englishness). To do so they embrace a new identity that gives them a sacred legitimacy: Islam. To adopt "Muslim" as an identity means not having to be either French or Arab. Islam as an identity gives meaning to an existence crushed by that double denial and the exhausting reminder of a dual inadequacy. Young people of North African descent cannot be French because they are fundamentally "Arab," but they are Arab in name only. They do not speak Arabic, though often they know a few terms of abuse and have a rough understanding of dialectal Arabic, and they are considered foreigners in the country of their parents or grandparents. In Islam, they find a purpose in life. A few of them study it in greater depth and embrace it in earnest, but the majority remain uninformed about the religion they claim as the foundation of their identity. Victimhood is accompanied by a profoundly hopeless view of their social situation. In Europe, especially in France, getting a job and becoming a full-fledged citizen is much more difficult for a Mohamed—given the social and racial prejudice he faces and the dubious stereotypes he must combat—than for a Robert. Just the same, not all doors are closed. Some of these young people manage to obtain a higher education and join the middle classes in the city's "normal" neighborhoods. They then seek to blend in anonymously, carefully avoid alluding to where they come from, and above all sever their ties with those who have not succeeded in leaving the ghetto.

Victimhood is fueled by a turbulent history, especially for Algerians, who constitute the majority of migrants from North Africa: the war of independence, the tragic fate of the Harkis (Algerians who fought on the French side, thousands of whom were murdered), and the resentment of the million *pieds noirs* (Algerians of French descent) forced to flee Algeria, who, years later, must interact with those who denied them their right to live in the country they consider their homeland. Racism and a lack of understanding of the Maghrebis feed on that history, which in France has not had a happy outcome, unlike in South Africa, where commissions set up to overcome bitterness and resentment achieved national reconciliation. The third-generation descendants of Africans who immigrated to France, vulnerable to that sense of victimhood, face four options:

Blend into the Middle Classes and Face the Consequences
The first path is difficult and full of pitfalls. It is that of social and economic integration, which means fighting against prejudice and indignity by staying in school or taking a job and devoting oneself to it body and soul. Those who make that choice overcome victimhood

and adopt a more realistic view of society, learning to fight stereotypes with flexibility and adaptation instead of overaggressiveness and hatred. They must change their accent and stop yelling as they do with their friends, everyone trying to outdo the others in a verbal sparring match, the loudest voice being the most virile. They must change their look, abandon the back slang of the *banlieues* and speak plainly. Above all, they must avoid an aggressive tone and monosyllabic phrases and express themselves in a less *banlieue* French. They must also practice self-discipline, learn to be more punctual and "serious" than the average French person, thus paying a symbolic ransom for their Arab background. All that is very difficult, and the ones who succeed are those who have lived in intact families, where the father assists the mother in raising the children and in seeing that they study hard. The single-parent families common in ghetto neighborhoods are a major handicap, though some manage to overcome it with the support of a teacher or an organized community. Others will find, in their capacity for detachment, the strength to conquer their hatred of an unjust society and an unforgiving environment and to resist the siren call of criminality.

Those who manage to rise to the ranks of the middle classes often have only one thing on their minds: to move into town and live as anonymously as possible, forget the past and put behind them the friends and acquaintances who remind them of their confinement in the ghetto and their isolation from society. Once they have forgotten the bad neighborhoods, new vistas open up for them, but the abandoned districts are further weakened, because they are no longer able to count on those who have left. In other words, success is individualized, while the difficulties of exclusion and criminality are collectivized, imposing on the neighborhood its identity: it has a bad reputation (its residents are criminals), the schools are low-performing (the rate of success at exams is low, and the middle classes try to place their children elsewhere), those who live there are discredited in the eyes of employers, and unemployment is very high. Young people in these neighborhoods get up late and hang out in gangs, living isolated lives in a breeding ground for petty and serious crime.

That *hittisme* and *trabendisme* (hanging out and trafficking in illegal goods) are fundamental for boys.[4] On the streets, young men may find themselves in contact with new versions of Islam, including rigorist and ultraorthodox Salafism. Within these faiths, a form of sectarian sociability takes root, in which one's difference from the larger society is experienced as a choice rather than passively endured. Young men very often consider their criminal way of life— drug dealing and stealing, or "steaming" in the lingo of the poor neighborhoods of Great Britain—to be inevitable. They are persuaded that they have no other choice if they are to escape and join the wealthier classes, at least through consumerism. Islamization, by contrast, presents itself as an individual choice, distinct from family and associates, based on a new model. Choice being denied in other areas (work, school, neighborhood), individualization crystallizes in religiosity. The paradox is that sectarianism, especially in its Salafist form, is at odds with individuality. Nevertheless, religious radicalization overcomes these young men's sense that their fate (*mektub*) is unavoidable, because death becomes an essential aspect of individual "freedom." To opt for Islamic extremism is to reject the inevitability of the choice imposed by the neighborhood, others, and society. The new, inflexible faith releases individuals from the yoke of what they have always felt was a predetermined path, criminality included. Now they steal and deal drugs to finance holy war, not out of greed.

Embrace Criminality, Hatred, and Its Sacralization

The second path is to opt, willingly or by force of circumstance, for criminality, which may allow young men to live far above the standard of living of their environment. Easy money, shady dealings in disreputable spots, and violence against police and other gang leaders structure an existence that swings back and forth between prison and the high life afforded by drug dealing, theft, or other forms of commerce in the underground economy. That path is by far the easiest for the young men who roam the streets, rise late and retire late, and while away long hours with neighborhood pals, sharing the hope of escaping poverty through the magic of lawbreaking in a brotherhood of aggressive self-assertion. More or less unstable groups form around gang leaders who assert their authority with threats, violence, and the demand for "family" loyalty. "Big brothers" take advantage of legal minors, assigning them to conduct surveillance and sell drugs on the street. They give them a little money and paint a glowing picture of a future of fast cars, brand-name shoes, and other perks of an expensive lifestyle, when their young charges will be able to invite their pals to upscale restaurants and help their parents or other members of the family move back home to the North African *bled*. Criminality is an attempt to bypass low-paying jobs and gain direct access to middle-class status, under the nose of a society that hates these young people and which they hate just as much. In that desire to live and consume like the wealthy classes, there is a thirst for revenge and provocation against a society—and also its administration and institutional authorities— where they almost always feel like despised intruders. In criminality, hatred of society is expressed nonideologically, in egoistic terms: subjects do not seek to change the world, but rather to improve their own lot in defiance of the forces that prevent them from achieving the status of the rich. Not only do they violate the laws, but they also taunt "honest people," who are themselves poorly paid but try to impose norms that reduce these young people to insignificance and block their access to consumer goods. There is provocation in that act, but its transgressiveness expresses a desire to improve their lot at all costs.

Victimhood has another consequence: in forming a narcissistic attachment to their own pain, young people become insensitive to the suffering of others. In that sense, victimhood justifies violence by taking away the capacity to feel guilt. Given that society has closed all its doors, it becomes legitimate to take revenge on any of its members, and there is no longer a place for remorse or guilt.

When the hatred of society brought on by victimhood becomes sanctified by Islam, these young people go even further. Islam becomes the expression of a mythic continuity with parents. It is placed on a pedestal and is experienced—even by those who are not observant Muslims—as exempt from the indignity they feel in a society that denies them their due. As a result, it becomes their fundamental referent, the bearer of all that is not "tainted," of the sacred—both because it is a religion and because it is not French or English. More broadly, it is not marred by Western civilization, which is considered a source of evil because it has always been anti-Islamic. For that hostile world, where they are held back as individuals and as Muslims, these young people no longer feel compassion. Radical Islamism gives rise to an easy conscience and an absence of guilt, even for the worst violence. Terrorists can kill without a guilty conscience because the misdeeds inflicted on Muslims justify revenge on anyone— Christian, Jewish, Muslim, or other—who does not share the radical point of view.

Such was the case for Zacarias Moussaoui and Mohamed Merah. Once the victimized are radicalized, a mythified Islam allows for an escalation of violence extending to the entire collectivity. Without jihadism, the victimized young commit violence with no remorse against those who get in their way. Once they have embraced religious extremism, violence becomes the royal road to self-realization as knights of faith against a godless world. Radicalization through religion exhorts them to perpetrate endless violence in the name of a pure faith, the realization of which entails eliminating those who embody unbelief.

Take the Sectarian Path

The third path leads to "internal exile." Subjects cut themselves off from society by embracing forms of Islamic identity that provide inner peace at the cost of isolation within a more or less sectarian universe. They become Salafists or, less often, members of Tablighi Jamaat (Society for Spreading Faith). They mock consumer society and sever their ties with the external world. They are passionate about cultivating their faith away from a corrupt world that takes no heed of death or piety and promotes frivolous consumerism and sexual perversion, as if life ended here below and there were no God or Satan, no paradise or hell. Hatred of society is transformed into a sense of internalized spiritual superiority, the self-righteousness of "the chosen" facing down the slaves of pleasure and life in this material world. Violence is exorcized thanks to a change in the reference group, which is no longer society and its norms but the closed group and its prohibitions. New forms of sociability make their appearance. Subjects marry by preference within the group, and women accept unequal treatment in the name of their faith. Converts vie with one another in their zeal to learn the language of the Prophet and to memorize suras from the Quran, which they readily quote in Arabic, not without a hint of exhibitionism, to highlight the importance of the verses and enhance their own status in the eyes of other Muslims, who may have doubts about the authenticity of the newcomers' faith.

Above all, they strive to put into practice in their everyday lives the sayings of the Prophet (the Hadith), duly recorded by several generations of Muslim traditionists, to acquire legitimacy in the eyes of novices or those who might see their conversion as religious consumerism tinged with exoticism. In that pietistic one-upmanship, they attempt to codify everything, down to the slightest detail of everyday life, with reference to the Quran or Hadith. Their existence, formerly unstructured and filled with anxiety, becomes regimented by time, the five calls to prayer giving each day the same shape and consistency. Religious rules, which govern even how to wash and groom themselves, become reassuring markers for the unemployed, who lack the social frame of reference that a job provides, or those so financially insecure that they no longer feel like part of the world. The closed group surrounds them with norms and prescriptions. It confers a sacred meaning on life, now structured by prayers and prohibitions, the violation of which is not illegal but impious. Life expands to include the hereafter, and the major concern is to ensure a happy afterlife through meritorious acts.

In the overwhelming majority of cases, becoming one of these pietistic "chosen" prevents recourse to violence. These subjects do not seek to change the godlessness of the world they live in. At best, their goal is to emigrate—as the Prophet did from Mecca to Medina—to Islamic countries where they will be able to live their faith without suffering the social disapproval attached to Islam in France. There the men can wear full beards, jellabas, and qamises, and the women niqabs. They can all say their prayers in broad daylight without being accused of religious extremism. They can devote themselves to a pious life without being exposed to images of naked women and sexual promiscuity, especially between people of the same sex, and they can shield their children from the attraction of alcohol and other drugs prohibited by Islam. In short, they can live in accordance with the ideal of Islamic orthodoxy, the practice of which is more difficult in the land of godlessness. Fundamentalists, whether Salafists or members of Tablighi Jamaat, feel at ease with themselves as part of a religious elite who live their faith intensely, at a remove from the larger society. In the overwhelming majority of cases, they do not seek to fight the godless West with weapons, but live there as a stopgap measure, unable to settle in Islamic regions.

Choose Sacred Violence and the Status of Negative Hero

The fourth option for the victimized young is violent warfare against France (or, more broadly, the West), in the name of the urgent imperative of their faith. This time, the rift with society is not achieved peacefully through adherence to a sectarian version of Islam in which individuals seek to protect themselves from the outside world by hardening their symbolic shells. Instead, it is achieved through sacred violence whose categorical imperative is war against the West. Society is rotten to the core, and there is no individual salvation apart from violent confrontation, to save Muslims and stop perversion on all sides by a secularized vision that, in the name of popular sovereignty, denies the power of God and His commandments. According to this point of view, democratic idolatry consists of substituting for God the will of a people blinded by its alienation and the manipulation of perverse elites. The solution to victimhood is then found in sacred violence: not only does no individual strategy allow subjects to escape, but any attitude that would forgo holy war is null and void. Nevertheless, these young people must manage to convince themselves that authentic Islam advocates violence and that that path is the only legitimate one. To do so, they have two invaluable sources: the Internet, where they can find ideological documents justifying jihad; and circles of other young people who, often outside the mosques and in more or less underground associations, glorify sacred violence as the sole solution to the ills suffered by Muslims and, more generally, by humanity held hostage to the forces of evil incarnated in the illegitimate powers of the Crusaders who rule the world.

On the Internet, young people find an abundance of works by the leading lights of contemporary jihadism. There are about ten radical

Arab ideologues,[5] supported by many "minor intellectuals," who serve as amplifiers and transmit their messages, vulgarizing them to make them accessible to followers not versed in the arcana of Muslim theology and law. That literature has been translated into English almost in its entirety (some of it into French as well) and is available on various jihadist sites, which, though monitored by Western law enforcement, are not banned, given that indoctrination is not considered a crime.

Nevertheless, other ingredients are necessary for a portion (a very small portion) of young Muslims from immigrant backgrounds, along with others who have converted to Islam, to be able to identify with that type of ideology. For some, the idea that the horizon of the future is blocked and that Muslims are under pressure by virtue of an insurmountable animosity between the Islamic world and the West serves as an escape route from victimhood. In daily life, they say, citing the prohibition of the hijab, the rejection of Islamic norms, and the spread of secularism, Muslims are stigmatized and put on notice to renounce their faith.

The essential elements of the new religious extremism are an anti-imperialist and antisecularist discourse and a patriarchal viewpoint (the differences between men and women must be reinstated in the name of the faith). If that vision is to appeal to the young, most of them disinherited and excluded from the economy, it must somehow promise individual advancement. Fulfillment comes through the status of "negative hero." The young who embrace victimhood believe they have exhausted all paths for escaping social insignificance. Henceforth, it is no longer success that motivates them but the universal acknowledgment of their war with society. Their aim is no longer integration via positive avenues but rather the negative recognition afforded by fear and anxiety. Instead of being respected, these negative heroes must be feared as a threat, a "scourge," a lurking presence who attracts attention by means of terror. These victimized young, most of them men, believe they are incapable of becoming positive heroes; that is evident in their daily lives, which lack the slightest possibility for self-fulfillment. If they commit a "sensational" act as jihadists, from one day to the next they will acquire the envied status of a star with an international reputation. What does it matter if they are described in negative terms, considered fanatics, hated? They will be famous; they will have escaped insignificance. They will count, will no longer be nobodies. They take pride in causing fear, like Merah. They are righters of wrongs who brandish the saber of Islam against enemies and, through the use of violence, symbolically reestablish the equilibrium long skewed in favor of the West. Their violent acts damn their adversaries, who will go to hell, but are redemptive for the jihadists. If they die along with many infidels, they will acquire the status of martyrs and go to paradise. In all cases, they are bound to win, because they enjoy an enormous advantage: they are not afraid of death—may even come to desire it—whereas their pusillanimous enemies fear it above all else. That attitude confers an undeniable moral superiority on jihadists. They have gone from being inferior to being superior; previously looked down on, they recover their dignity through the fear they inspire in their former denigrators. From the loathing others feel for them, negative heroes draw reasons to feel that they are better than everyone else.

Negative heroes revel in the fear they inspire and the attention of the media. The more they are denounced, the more reason they find for glory, by squandering the only goods they possess (before they are stopped): other people's lives and, as a last resort, their own, which they are ready to sacrifice for the holy cause. Their death will seal a fate that purports to be meaningful, in the face of a society they demonized and that demonizes them. Once the final degree of radicalization has been reached—the assumption of the status of negative hero—no further dialogue can occur. The outcome of the conflict is decided solely by death inflicted or suffered.

The malaise of the victimized young resulting from marginalization may extend to members of the Muslim middle class, in the form of identity wounds. Suffering from anonymity and a life marked by anomie (they no longer feel part of a community, social bonds are broken, and they bear the burden of a meaningless existence), they become self-proclaimed spokespersons for what other Muslims suffer: imperialism, Zionism, and Western repression. Because they are middle class, they are even less tolerant of the stigmatization and prejudice faced by Islam and its followers. Having become self-proclaimed defenders of Islam in a world where they no longer have to prove themselves, the radicalized from the middle classes, unlike the young outcasts, do not even need to turn inferiority into superiority through their cruel acts, for they are already among the "superior."

Individuals from the middle classes may become involved in jihadism for want of an identity solidly based in the real, as the consequence of an anomie that reaches to the core of their existence. So it is that some individuals with stacks of degrees in the exact sciences, members of major international scientific institutions, opt for struggle in the name of holy war to aid Islam. Having lost all sense of reality, living in a world where the virtual can encroach on the real, they may play the negative hero on jihadist sites, establishing contacts, encrypting messages, serving as intermediaries under various names and pseudonyms: in short, combining fiction and reality in an oneiric holy war that can exact a high price and have damaging consequences for themselves and others.[6] These quixotic knights of the apocalypse, assuming the half-dream, half-real personalities of irresolute slayers, play a dangerous game with their own identities and with their interlocutors, fictional and real. If they find an opportunity and meet a group that supports them, they may go a long way. Such a group may give them real resources for their ambition (to learn to handle arms and explosives, to escape their comfort zone and join a group of fighters) and may inspire in them a hatred of society, by associating the wounds attributable to the imperialist and colonial past of their adopted country with present-day policy (the invasion of Afghanistan, Iraq, Mali, and other countries). But often these middle-class subjects lack the determination of jihadists from the working classes, who seek to avenge their own suffering.

The anomic character of middle-class jihadism in the West is not replicated in Muslim societies. There, the indignation at being marginalized or excluded from the political and economic arenas by corrupt and autocratic ruling elites produces a resentment rooted not in identity but in dreadful daily reality. Radicalization therefore does not assume unreal forms but becomes the very language of people grappling with an unforgiving reality, blacklisted in their very existence and reduced to a profound indignity by a power devoid of legitimacy.

Negative heroes often straddle several cultures at once. In their way, they are multiculturalists, though they deny having any culture other than that prescribed by Islam, namely, submission to the commandments of Allah in a universalism that negates all cultural specificity. One example will aptly demonstrate that type of straddling. In Woolwich, a neighborhood in southeast London, two black converts of Nigerian descent killed a British soldier with machetes on May 29, 2013. Michael Adebolajo, twenty-nine, who calls himself Mujahid Abu Hamza, and his accomplice, Michael Adebowale, twenty-two (Ismail Ibn Abdullah, to use his Islamic name), had premeditated the murder and obtained the large knives the day before. The leader, Adebolajo, had composed a last will and testament of holy death (martyrdom), which read, "To my children, whom I love, know that fighting the enemies of Allah is a religious obligation." The two men chose a soldier, as Merah would also do, because, according to them, members of the military are on the front lines of the battle against Islam. They watched him as he left the Woolwich barracks, dressed in civilian clothes but wearing a military pack, chased him down in a car, crashed into him, then stabbed him repeatedly and tried to decapitate him, without entirely succeeding. Afterward, brandishing a rusty weapon in a kind of playacting, they waited for the police, hoping to be killed as martyrs. They were only wounded, then arrested.

The two men converted to Islam in the early 2000s. The older of them had until that time been attending mass regularly and was also influenced by the Jehovah's Witnesses. After his conversion to Islam, he joined the extremist group al-Muhajiroun (the Emigrants), now banned, and listened to the sermons of Omar Bakri, one of the prominent ideologues of "Londonistan." The war in Iraq and the British army's involvement in it shocked Adebolajo deeply. He could not bear the complicity of the press, which praised Western intervention even though Muslims were being killed. In London he participated in protest movements against the war in 2006, 2007, and 2009. He attempted to leave for Somalia to join the Islamist forces of al-Shabaab in 2012, but was arrested in Kenya and sent back to Great Britain. The British secret intelligence service, MI5, identified him as an Islamist in 2006 for having participated in violent demonstrations against the police, and he was placed on a watch list of three thousand terrorists when he attempted to leave for Somalia. There is a similarity here to the case of Mohamed Merah, whom the French Renseignements Généraux (General Intelligence) had also identified as a radical Islamist but whom they allowed to go free. Both men attacked soldiers, a common target in such cases, and were mentally unstable, a recurrent trait among the new types of jihadists.

The other member of the team, Adebowale, twenty-two, had led a chaotic life. From the age of fourteen he was a member of a gang; he became a drug trafficker, was injured in a brawl, and served an eight-month prison sentence. Like many jihadists, he suffered from major psychological disorders. After doing time, he severed ties with his family and converted to Islam. During his arrest after the murder of the soldier, Lee Rigby, he became violent, spitting on police officers and assaulting them.[7]

These two men were acculturated to radicalism by means of antisocial symbols. The elder one declared, "Al-Qaeda, I consider them mujahedeen. I love them, they're my brothers. I've never met them, but I consider them my brothers in Islam. . . . The mujahedeen are the army of Allah."[8] He glorified al-Qaeda as fighters in the holy war against the West, where Michael Adebolajo had long lived and where he converted to Islam. His self-constitution as a negative hero and his idolization of the group with which he identified thus occurred on the basis of an acculturation that Georges Devereux has called *antagonistic*. The symbolism of the murder is significant. After killing the English soldier, Adebolajo, his hands red with blood, brandished the machete in front of the cameras in an attitude of defiance, sending a warning to any Britons who would take it into their heads to provoke Muslims. That gesture can be seen as an imitation of Islamic paradigms (like slitting the soldier's throat, as Omar Bakri recommended in his sermons). But the symbolism was double-edged: it could have come from the pages of the al-Qaeda magazine *Inspire* or from jihadist videos, which show ad nauseam scenes of butchery and the slaughter of heretics, but it also could have come from rap videos filmed in southeast London.[9] That symbolism is at the crossroads between homegrown terrorism and transnational jihadism. Negative heroes "cobble together" cultural mélanges, even when they claim to be conforming to the strict letter of jihad, beyond cultural particularities.

In Western societies, the vast majority of people perceive negative heroes (or "human bombs") as merciless fanatics without a conscience, monsters. Aspiring negative heroes experience their monstrosity as a positive trait precisely because of their antagonistic acculturation. The more the "godless" society hates them, the surer they are of their status as heroes for the imagined Islamic society on whose behalf they wish to martyr themselves. Other people's hatred reinforces their feeling of superiority. Negative heroes are heroes only in their own eyes; for everyone else, they are dehumanized fanatics.

FROM THE OLD RADICALIZED TO THE NEW

The past decade has seen a modification in the forms of radicalization visible in Europe. Behaviors have changed, as have relations among individuals, especially in the public space. To simplify, I shall distinguish the "classic" form, dating to the late twentieth century and the first years of the twenty-first, from the new, much more complex form that has emerged in the last few years.

In the classic model, the behavior of individuals undergoing radicalization was similar to that of religious fundamentalists, who have no connection per se to jihadism. That similarity was the source of both the strength and the weakness of jihadists. They shared with religious fundamentalists the following traits:

- The men wore full beards, which distinguished them from non-Muslims but also from "bad Muslims," even "apostates"—those they considered renegades for not conforming to Islamic prescriptions, as interpreted by the ultraorthodox. Islamic fundamentalists often call themselves Salafists, in reference to the Salaf, the Prophet's companions and the first few generations of Muslims, who, according to them, respected his commandments. Jihadists are often called Salafist jihadists by all sides.
- They behaved aggressively toward non-Muslims and toward Muslims who did not follow their radical version of Islam.

- They challenged "moderate" imams who did not embrace the radical vision.
- They dressed in jellabas and qamises like the Salafists, who think they are emulating the Prophet. They used a *siwak* (a wooden toothbrush made from a twig of the *Salvadora persica* tree, of the type the Prophet supposedly used) instead of its modern equivalent. They did all this in the public space in a deliberately conspicuous way, to attract followers from among "lukewarm" Muslims or to encourage by example the conversion of non-Muslims.
- Radicalized converts adopted an ultraorthodox attitude and accordingly rejected all who did not conform to their vision of Islam. Their attitude was different from that of other Muslims: they were obliged to display greater zeal to be accepted by their new coreligionists, who were still a little skeptical of their sincerity. Ultraorthodoxy fostered a sense of brotherhood despite the "whites" or "colonialists" associated with their preconversion French past.
- They developed a form of proselytism not confined to Muslims (in contrast to the usual practice among the followers of Tablighi Jamaat) but also addressing Christians and even atheists. They constituted groups of five, six, or more to engage in a conspicuous promotion of an Islam at odds with secular norms, deliberately provoking uneasiness in those who witnessed it.
- They promoted religious activities, especially during the month of Ramadan, the aim being to make Muslims who did not strictly observe the fast feel guilty, and also urged them to perform the five daily prayers in full. Often they tried to more or less force other members of their families to follow their intransigent model of religion.

- They appropriated specific religious terminology, high-lighting such notions as *kufr* ("unbelief" or "heresy," depending on the context), *jahiliyya* ("ignorance," a reference to the pre-Islamic period but also to the current era, when many Muslims and non-Muslims continue to be ignorant of or to reject fundamentalist Islam), and *jihad* (holy war against the infidels but also against illegitimate Islamic governments that represent global idolatry, or *taqut*.

These behaviors, followed to a greater or lesser extent by fundamentalists (especially by what are known as peaceful or "scientific" Salafists), were shared by jihadists until the early 2000s.

It should be noted that most fundamentalists are not jihadists, but that, before the attacks of September 11, 2001, and even for a few years afterward, most jihadists exhibited conspicuous behavior similar to that of the fundamentalists. In fact, that attitude made it easier for the police to identify them. Such was the case, for example, for a group from the nineteenth arrondissement in Paris that was dismantled in early 2005. Around its leader Farid Benyettou, the group recruited volunteers to wage jihad in Iraq. Its members attracted the attention of the police when, among other things, they demonstrated against the law prohibiting the Islamic headscarf in public schools, thus publicly displaying their adherence to ultraorthodox Islam. Until even a few years ago, that combination of public fundamentalism and a radical vision of Islam was the dominant form of radicalization, despite warnings from major ideologues of jihad, such as Abu Mus'ab al-Suri, who urged partisans of holy war to conceal their religious identity.

A jihadist branch of fundamentalist Salafism appeared in the 1990s. Though sectarian in their attitudes, Salafists had not previously advocated violence in the name of holy war. Traditional *sheikhi* ("scientific") Salafism sought—and still seeks—to spread Islam through morals and customs, not jihad. It avoids politicization and violence, opting instead for *da'wa* (proselytism, the call to join Islam). Radical jihadist Salafism called for the application of Sharia through the use of warfare, either to recover Islamic lands conquered by the infidels (Palestine and Afghanistan, then Iraq, invaded by the U.S. and British armies, and now Mali, by the French) or, in the case of the "Qutbist current" (named after Sayyid Qutb, ideologue of the Muslim Brotherhood), to advance the cause of Islam throughout the world.

Until the first years of the twenty-first century, partisans of jihadist Salafism thought that, in the West, where Islam is a minority religion, it was necessary to display their religious zeal and adopt a fundamentalist posture to attract the young, whether de-Islamized, "born again," or in the process of conversion. Those who became radicalized let their beards grow out and proudly exhibited their adherence to the religion of Allah. They embraced the form of proselytism typical of Muslims who have rediscovered their faith in a militant form, marking themselves off from their parents, whose religious practice was an "orthopraxy" (ritualist practice) lacking any ideological vision. The ideologization of Islam went hand in hand with a restored pride, a feeling of superiority over traditional Muslims and secularists, who did not understand the meaning of the religion. Conspicuousness was an integral part of the new religiosity, which needed to distinguish itself symbolically from both backward-looking Muslims (parents and grandparents) and a French society imbued with secular values, which fundamentalists identified with antireligiosity (true, in fact, for a minority of secularists).

That model underwent a radical change a few years after the September 11 attacks, especially when followers of Islamic extremism became aware of the growing surveillance being conducted on them by the intelligence services.

THE INTROVERTED MODEL OF JIHADISM

For the past few years a new, more introverted model of radicalization has been emerging. Fundamentalist Islam continues to recruit a few believers who later separate themselves from networks that are not activist enough for their taste and join more belligerent groups, but the great majority do not take that step. Nowadays, most of those who become radicalized opt for an introverted attitude, concealing their faith to escape the police and intelligence services. Whether converts or "born again" Muslims, they shave their beards and do everything they can to blend in.

Furthermore, the new radical extremists work in small networks rather than large groups. Since the London attacks in July 2005, attempts by networks of more than three or four people to carry out a terrorist action have ended in failure almost everywhere in Europe. The intelligence or police services intercepted their cell phone or Internet communications. By contrast, attacks by individuals (such as Mohamed Merah and Anders Breivik) and by microgroups, whether in the name of radical Islam or some other cause, could not be prevented. It seems that terrorist attacks in the West are no longer likely to succeed unless they are committed by solitary individuals self-radicalized on the Web or by a tiny group. Of course, the singleton acts alone only in relative terms: he is more or less influenced by fundamentalist networks or groups. (Merah, for example, is said to have been influenced by the Forsane Alizza association.) But he takes action alone, unlike the usual pattern until 2005. Nineteen participants were directly involved in the attacks of September 11, 2001, four in the London attack of July 2005. But it is now primarily the lone wolf or the microgroup, acting in the name of a larger community—the Islamic Ummah, the nation, or the white man—that must be reckoned with.

The third trait characteristic of the new terrorists is their mental impairment or psychological fragility. Formerly, group dynamics kept psychologically fragile individuals from joining the plot. For example, Zacarias Moussaoui was eliminated from the circle that conducted the attack of September 11, 2001, because he was unreliable. Now that the decision to take action is made by a single individual or a group of two or three, mental illness has become a more important factor. It seems to have played a role in the actions of Mohamed Merah, Anders Breivik, Michael Adebowale, and Michael Adebolajo. Abdelhakim Dekhar's armed assault on journalists in the offices of BFM-TV and *Libération* in Paris in mid-November 2013 does not seem to have been a direct result of psychopathology, but he too seems to have acted alone.

To summarize the new forms of radicalization, in contrast to the classic profile described above, the following characteristics may be identified:

- A short beard or total absence of beard for the men, in contrast to the more or less bushy beards of fundamentalists.
- A refusal to build large-scale networks, for fear that they will be identified by the police.
- Rejection of all contact with "moderate" imams in the mosques, who are perceived as untrustworthy.
- An introverted attitude, especially in interactions with others. By renouncing proselytism and not allowing anyone else into the very small group (two or three people), the radical sacrifices conspicuousness and the legitimacy it confers among other Muslims in favor of concealment.
- A relationship between a strong personality, the "radicalizer," and an easily influenced, weak personality, often with psychological deficiencies, the "radicalized."
- Avoidance of any religious markers during Ramadan, particularly among converts, who often manage to hide their conversion from those around them.

- Teams of two or, more rarely, three persons, which are now the most common type of "radicalized networks."

Although that new type of radicalization is more difficult to neutralize, it also has less capacity to do harm. Until November 2014, with the exception of the massacre of Utøya by Anders Breivik in 2011, every successful attack caused "only" a few deaths.

SOLITARY, SELF-RADICALIZED INDIVIDUALS

The self-radicalized are those who become radicalized individually, under the influence of an association that reinforces their martial credo but without participating in their terrorist action, or through the Web, by reading radical works on the Internet or communicating with fundamentalists who instill in them the soul of a jihadist without joining a terrorist network or becoming involved in attacks themselves. Radicalization occurs gradually (sudden radicalization has not been verified in any concrete case), with occasional episodes of doubt: individuals at first maintain their aloofness, cobbling together ideologies from more or less radicalized sites but not establishing ties with anyone to constitute networks that would act in concert.

The term *lone wolf* describes a person who acts alone in perpetrating an attack but is influenced by a group or association that does not intervene directly. Mohamed Merah, who committed the attacks in Toulouse and Montauban in March 2012, and the convert "Alexandre," who wounded a soldier conducting a Vigipirate patrol in the district of La Défense in May 2013, meet that definition.

FROM THE PRERADICALIZED TO THE SUPERRADICALIZED

The European, and more broadly Western, model of radicalization has evolved since the late twentieth century. Whereas the radicalized involved in the September 11 attacks all came from the Middle East (most were Saudis or Egyptians), the twenty-first century has ushered in the era of homegrown terrorists, whose radicalization occurred through "buddies" and the Internet, but less and less through the radical groups of the Muslim world.

A new form of radicalization can be seen in Syria. Most of the young Europeans who go there (via Turkey especially) are not radicalized in the strict sense of the term when they set off. Their motivations are on the whole a poisonous mix of three components: humanitarian concerns (save the Muslim brothers being massacred by the bloody Assad regime), extreme fundamentalism (fight the Shia regime, which resulted from an adulterated Islam and which re-presses authentic Muslims, the Sunni), and a certain playfulness, associated with danger and the exoticism of a change of scene. A dilution of identity combines with the will to assert oneself as a Mus-lim hero even while having some fun, like adolescents who believe they are immortal and flirt with death. Jihadism has a tragic dimen-sion (anomic despair and an identity crisis) but also a comic side (raptures before the great unknown, one's own death and that of others). That comic aspect can be glimpsed especially when these young people go out at night to a makeshift cybercafé in a war-torn neighborhood in Syria. Cell phone in one hand, rifle in the other, they get their friends to take pictures of them, with no concern to conceal where they are staying, thus breaking the most elementary rules of discipline for that type of civil war (Thomson 2014). The sometimes irresponsible attitude of these young self-proclaimed sol-diers of Allah, toward both their own safety and that of the groups they claim to be part of, points to an adrenaline rush and the joy of adventure rather than the iron discipline of militiamen immured in their deadly creed.

Jihadist identity is reinforced by a complete break from daily life, which is not always unappealing to these French young people, a growing number of whom come from the lower middle classes or even from relatively comfortable classes. Sometimes they sever their ties with a more or less secure life to prove their sincerity to God, finding in that impulse the resources for a new identity reinvigorated by the sacred. Alienated individuals develop a relationship to God that authenticates them in their own eyes. They find a meaning to their existence and, by waging war against the enemy of Islam and against their own "materialistic" tendencies, they achieve a new kind of happiness. In fact, compared to the young people from the *banlieue*, who are outcast and feed on society's hatred, new followers have a much more conflicted relation to society. Their quest to wage war on the enemy has a religious meaning that is not synonymous with rejection of French society. They leave for Syria to redeem themselves in the eyes of Allah and to build a new identity, in which becoming heroes, courting death, and enduring the ordeals of the battlefield confer nobility on their undertaking. Their new sincerity finds a horizon of hope: death on the battlefield is transformed into martyrdom, and the departure from this world opens prospects for happiness in the next.

In that project of self-rehabilitation and self-reconstruction to conform to the norms of the sacred, women occupy an increasingly significant place. They are a minority, to be sure, but their numbers are growing. They dream of an imaginary matri-patriarchy, in which they would surpass the men even while subordinating themselves, renouncing the drabness of an increasingly prosaic feminism that has provided approximate equality within the context of absolute disenchantment. Men in the West often become radicalized out of castration anxiety (the equality of men and women deprives them of identity markers in both private and public life). By contrast, anxiety about the leveling effect of gender equality motivates women to accept their femininity as an inferiority, which they attempt magically to transmute into a new, meaningful life. Their departure for the

Syrian front takes the paradoxical form of a radicalization in which they renounce equality to build a new world steeped in the sacred. Jihadist women are also intent on demonstrating a kind of equality in death. If they can die as martyrs like the men, then equality ought to prevail in life as well, even in the heart of the imaginary Islam for which they hope and pray.

Some of these young people have been indoctrinated before leaving for Syria, via the Internet[10] or through charismatic individuals who vaunted the Syrian adventure,[11] but that does not mean they have been "jihadized," in the strong sense of the term. If that were the case, they would have acted like Khaled Kelkal in 1995 or Mohamed Merah in 2012: they would have attempted to perpetrate terrorist acts in France or Europe. At least in the case of the adults, they can be compared to the European and American "revolutionaries" or "republicans" who went to fight alongside the anti-Franco forces in the Spanish Civil War of 1936–1939; to leftists in the 1970s who joined Palestinian extremist groups; or to the Japanese leftists who in May 1972 attacked Lod Airport in Tel Aviv, killing twenty-six and injuring eighty, after a period of cooperation between the Japanese Red Army and extremists in Lebanon.

Young people are not motivated to leave for Syria solely by an identity crisis or a sense that something is missing from their lives. They are also expressing a revolutionary romanticism. The bankruptcy of left-wing radicalism and the end of revolutionary secular ideologies opened the way for radical Islam, which is by turns anti-imperialist and male chauvinist and antidemocratic. The first aspect satisfies those who see Western imperialism as part of the colonial legacy and the "white man's" arrogance. The second speaks to an identity crisis on the part of those who find no hope in the drabness of their European lives. "Leaving" is experienced as a leap into the unknown, an attempt to achieve happiness through the ideal of warfare. The promise of jihad on Syrian soil may be, in the words of a few young Britons who set off under the banner of ISIS, a "cure for the depression" gnawing away at the young.[12]

As a result, it is necessary to emphasize both dimensions at once—revolutionary romanticism and identity crisis—if we are to understand the complex motivations of young people who succumb to the Syrian temptation.[13]

These young people have a militant predisposition that can be called prejihadist, but they are a long way from embracing the violent creed of proven jihadists, who do not hesitate to kill innocents at home in the name of Allah.

The new phenomenon, when compared to the civil war in Spain or 1970s leftism, is the presence of minors, both boys and girls. It is much easier for these manipulated (and self-manipulated) youngsters[14] to leave for Turkey than it was for minors to get to Spain in the 1930s. To set their plans in motion, all they have to do now is buy an airplane ticket and extort a little money from parents or "borrow" it from friends. Among minors, the revolutionary dimension is by far overshadowed by adolescent malaise and an identity crisis: an "other" world appears preferable to one where they no longer know who is a friend and who an enemy, where the everyday has no noble message or promise of a happiness shared with others.

Once in Syria, the preradicalized become superradicalized, in contact with groups such as al-Nusra Front and especially ISIS, whose cruelty far surpasses even that of al-Qaeda. For several weeks, the young people take classes in ideology and train in zones of intense conflict. They are taught combat and bomb-making techniques on the ground; above all, they learn to sacrifice themselves for the cause of holy war. Their initial motivations, a mixture of humanitarian compassion and the desire to defend their Sunni brothers against Assad's heretical Shia regime, are transformed under the influence of a hyperbolic radicalization. In Syria, they become jihadists in the strict sense of the term.

As a result, their return to Europe poses extreme dangers. These young people are in fact superradicalized, having experienced total war in Syria and learned on the job a cruelty justified by dehumanizing religious ideals, with the psychological distortions they entail. They have learned to be much more insensitive to the suffering of others than the homegrown jihadists who imperfectly mastered techniques on the Web for making homemade bombs and perpetrated violent acts in Europe in the first decade of the 2000s. The superradicalized are even more battle-hardened than the "Afghans," the European or Arab jihadists who participated in the war against the Soviet Union in Afghanistan. Their number (more than two thousand Europeans and at least as many Maghrebis, some of whom will come to Europe), their resentment against a West that has done nothing to counter Assad's bloody regime in Syria, as well as their technical skill (waging direct war, making bombs) and virulent ideological indoctrination mean that they are among the major internal threats Europe will have to face in the decade to come, on both the human and the political levels. Moreover, the European far-right movements will use them as an argument to challenge European humanism and its open political system.

TYPES OF RADICALIZATION

Two types of radicalization can be distinguished: *ad extra* (directed outward) and *ad intra* (directed inward). In the first case, jihadists leave for another country, seeking to make holy war for religious or ideological reasons. There are hundreds of French people currently in Syria fighting the Assad regime in radical Islamist groups. And back in 2004–2005, twenty-four-year-old Farid Benyettou convinced a dozen young French of Maghrebi or African descent from the nineteenth arrondissement in Paris to go fight the American invader in Iraq. Some were killed, others were arrested by the U.S. Army, and others simply vanished. In contrast, domestic terrorists attack in the country where they live, from within. Such was the case, notably, for Mohamed Merah in France, for the Tsarnaev brothers, perpetrators of the Boston Marathon attacks in April 2013, and for the Britons Michael Adebolajo and Michael Adebowale, who killed a soldier in Woolwich.

Another major distinction can be made between national and transnational radicalization. National radicalization is grounded in a precise target, the enemy that occupies a country or is fighting national forces: the Indian army occupying Kashmir from the nationalists' point of view, or the Israeli army occupying Palestine, or the Russian army occupying the Caucasus or invading Chechnya, and so on. Its ultimate aim is to liberate national territory from the occupier's yoke. This radicalization is not "absolute"; it does not seek to fight a faceless global enemy, but rather targets a specific enemy with relatively well-defined traits. In the Islamist sphere, Hamas's enemy is the Israeli army, not humankind as a whole. By contrast, transnational radicalization (Islamist in this case) identifies a multifarious adversary with infinite variations: the United States, the Arab governments supported by it, the West and its humanism, the Shia, the Crusaders and Zionists real and imaginary, and all those whose religion is not Abrahamic, to whom jihadists would deny religious freedom. In a word, the enemy is the world, and death as a martyr is glorified. The killing has no end, because radicalization means "permanent revolution"—except that the religious dimension introduces male-female and believer-infidel relations that go far beyond a strictly revolutionary context. Jihadist radicalization stems from inextinguishable intransigence and hatred.

Nationalists who embrace Islam and jihad (Islamo-nationalists) are well aware that they must avoid cooperating with transnational Islamists of the al-Qaeda type. When they do cooperate, it is because they feel the national dimension has proven impossible to realize. That is particularly the case for the Palestinians of Lebanon, some of whom converted to transnational jihadism when they were removed from the Palestinian territories and subjected to the maelstrom of life in closed-off neighborhoods (Rougier 2004). In Kashmir, the close ties between Lashkar-e-Taiba and transnational jihadism can be attributed to the fact that the group was formed in Afghanistan in 1981 to fight the Communist regime and is close to the Taliban. In the 1990s that organization established itself in Kashmir, pushing for the Indian part of the province to be incorporated into Pakistan, an Islamic state. It has benefited from the support of al-Qaeda, thanks to its previous ties. It is subject to the same ambiguities as the Pakistani state and its powerful intelligence and security services, which sometimes cooperate with al-Qaeda, while at the same time being the ally of the United States in the fight against jihadist terrorism. That double game has been denounced by the U.S. intelligence services, to no avail. Palestinian movements, even Hamas and Islamic Jihad, have never cooperated with al-Qaeda, marking their distance from it by their relation to reality (the aim of national liberation) and their links to other nationalists.

By contrast, in the eyes of radical Islamists, nationalism is a form of heresy (*shirk*). In the shift from national to transnational, the nature of radicalization and the utopian dream change. The Islamo-nationalists are less rigorist than the jihadists; their aim is a version of Islam that promotes nationhood. Radical Islamists argue for Islamic hegemony beyond distinctions of nation or ethnicity. The only thing driving them is the myth of a universal Islamic state, the neocalifate, to be imposed on everyone by persuasion or force. Radicalization is limitless, because no concrete solution can be provided for an aspiration that is impossible to realize. The solution is death, and the aspiration to welcome it or inflict it is becoming the devouring passion of jihadists, who think they will find greater self-fulfillment the more unbelievers they kill and will find everlasting happiness by dying in the effort.

It is instructive to array a number of the attacks committed in recent years in a two-variable table, with the size of the groups on one axis and the nature of the attacks on the other (see Table 2).

The radicalization that takes place in democratic societies can also be distinguished from that which occurs in authoritarian states. Grievances and extremist ideologies can lead to radicalization in both cases, but the two types of political regime produce forms of radicalization that are utterly distinct in their scope and intensity, and also in the ways radicalized groups are constituted.

In the West, radicalized subjects constitute a tiny minority of the population, because of the open nature of the political system. Even the Muslim minority in European countries (between 2 and 8 percent of the population, depending on the country) is overwhelmingly opposed to jihadism, which leads jihadists to seek out groups of young delinquents who sympathize with them but usually do not take the next step and follow them.

By contrast, in authoritarian countries, the illegitimacy of the ruling power bestows a form of legitimacy on any opposition, even if it is violent, and jihadism makes use of that legitimacy to win the complicity of many strata of the population. In present-day Egypt, the government's repression of the Muslim Brotherhood has led some of its sympathizers to embrace jihadism and has lent legitimacy to the radical Islamists, who point out the failure of the Muslim Brotherhood's "peaceful Islam" and therefore resort to violence. The violence of the illegitimate state partly justifies the violence of Muslim extremists, and the number of their sympathizers is far higher there than in democratic societies, where dissension can be expressed in the political space.

In general, authoritarian powers give rise to an extremism on their periphery that takes root in the local population. An outlying population is doubly marginalized by the authorities, first, along with

Table 2. Types of Terrorist Attacks

	Singletons	Small groups (two or three members)	Groups with several members
Ad intra	Mohamed Merah; Nidal Malik Hasan	The Tsarnaev brothers; the two Britons of Nigerian descent Michael Adebolajo and Michael Adebowale	The "Roubaix gang" in France; al-Shabaab in Somalia, linked to al-Qaeda; al-Qaeda in the Islamic Maghreb (AQIM) in Algeria; al-Qaeda between the two rivers of Iraq; al-Nusra Front in Syria, which became a branch of al-Qaeda; Lashkar-e-Taiba in India (Kashmir)
Ad extra	European jihadists in Syria	The young people sent to Iraq by Farid Benyettou	September 11 attacks in the United States; attacks of July 2005 in London
Murder of targeted populations	Baruch Goldstein, member of the Kahanist group, who killed 29 Palestinians and injured 125 in 1994; Nidal Malik Hasan, who killed soldiers and assimilated groups at the Fort Hood military base; Mohamed Merah, who killed Muslim soldiers and Jewish civilians	Michael Adebolajo and Michael Adebowale, for the murder of an English soldier (the military)	Attacks in Bombay in November 2008 (where Lashkar-e-Taiba played an essential role) against a Jewish synagogue

Table 2. (*continued*)

	Singletons	Small groups (two or three members)	Groups with several members
Indiscriminate killing	Timothy McVeigh, who killed 168 and injured 680 in Oklahoma City on April 19, 1995 (he denounced the "tyrannical" government of the United States, but this was actually a massacre of anyone who was in the Alfred P. Murrah Federal Building)	The Tsarnaev brothers at the Boston Marathon	September 11 attacks; attacks of March 4, 2004, in Madrid; attacks of July 2005 in London
Limited utopianism		Two female Chechen suicide bombers, who blew themselves up at a rock music festival in Moscow on July 5, 2003 (15 dead, 60 injured); two female suicide bombers who blew themselves up in the Moscow subway on March 29, 2010, killing 39 and injuring 71	Palestinian, Chechen, Kashmiri, and other suicide bombers, who are motivated by nationalism
Frenzied utopianism	Mohamed Merah and most of the radical Islamists who have perpetrated attacks alone in Europe; Anders Breivik	Two female suicide bombers who blew themselves up in a market in Baghdad on February 1, 2008, probably at the instigation of al-Qaeda, killing 99	al-Qaeda and affiliated groups

civil society as a whole, and second, as periphery. For example, the radical Islamists of the Caucasus, under the leadership of Doku Umarov, seem to have been behind the two attacks perpetrated in Volgograd on December 29 and 30, 2013, which killed seventeen and injured about forty the first day, with fourteen dead and twenty-eight injured on the second. A portion of the Muslim population in these countries, where the government is repressive and utterly corrupt, sympathize with the radicalized who go underground (into the forest) to wage the fight. Such is not the case in western Europe, where even outcast and stigmatized Muslims in the *banlieues* or poor neighborhoods do not readily share the jihadist creed, though some grievances associated with Islamophobia and social rejection may spark a vague sympathy. In societies governed by authoritarian states, all citizens are in a sense victims of political exclusion and feel wronged. That is all the more true for Muslims, who may feel like second-class citizens not protected by the law and subject to the arbitrariness of the rulers. The jihadist phenomenon then takes on a scope it does not achieve in democratic societies, where citizens benefit from a much less arbitrary judicial system. By allowing free discourse, democracy may initially favor the birth of extremism, religious or otherwise, but works against it in the long run, if only because the revulsion and insecurity caused by terrorist acts unify people against those who practice it. In countries ruled by an autocracy (a number of Arab countries, Russia, and the Central Asian republics), public opinion is muzzled or unable to form in the first place, and therefore cannot exert a moderating influence on groups tempted by radical violence. Only the fear of a tyrannical state's violence can prevent extremism, but that can only be a negative factor. We are thus seeing a fresh outbreak of radicalized groups in regions such as the Russian Caucasus, where the Caucasus Emirate attracts young people and urges them to commit attacks not only in the region but also in

Moscow. The double attack in the Moscow subway in March 2010 caused forty deaths; the suicide attack at the Moscow Domodedovo Airport on January 24, 2011, thirty-seven.

THE ROLE OF FUNDAMENTALISM IN RADICALIZATION

Is fundamentalism the gateway to radicalization, or is it an obstacle to its implementation?

The forms that fundamentalism takes may be more or less rigid: the wearing of the burqa by some young women in defiance of the law, demands for accommodations for Islam or Judaism in the public space by followers of those religions, occasional proselytism by Pentecostals, or the fight by Jehovah's Witnesses for the right to refuse blood transfusions, even for their children in life-threatening situations. The degree of radicality in fundamentalism varies, depending on the religion and the national and international context. Religious violence is not at comparable levels among Catholics, Protestants, Jews, and Muslims.

In our time, there is no major propensity within Christianity for holy war. A minor trend of that type arose in Judaism in the 1970s–1990s, but it is practically absent from Europe in the early twenty-first century. Jihadist Islam is the only major religious current that advocates holy violence against the "godless." Statistically, that tendency has been unable to make significant inroads in Europe since 2005, but the threat still looms. Since that time, Islamic jihadists have perpetrated several mass murders in Europe and the United States.

Two main types of Islamic fundamentalism in Europe can be distinguished. Al-Tabligh wal-Da'wa (Faith and Practice Association), a transnational religious group whose headquarters are in Pakistan and which came into existence in the late 1920s, is one of the organizations that can be characterized as "fundamentalist" without any pejorative connotations. It practices a form of religiosity that

121

aspires to be totalizing, encompassing every dimension of the believer's existence and founded on the crucial importance of *da'wa*, or religious proselytism. The organization, which has branches everywhere in Europe, advocates a rigorist but apolitical vision of Islam, and its activism is limited to the call to faith, especially among "lukewarm" Muslims, who are lax in their religious practice. Small groups of members "tour" every week, particularly in the *banlieues* of France, calling for the young to join their ranks. Proselytism is aimed primarily at young people destined for prison, those from "disaffiliated" neighborhoods where delinquency and the flouting of social norms prevail. Tablighi Jamaat seeks to make these young people "born-again" Muslims, leading them to embrace voluntarily its version of the faith.

Another, much less organized group is the Salafists, whose members adhere to a shared religious identity in their rejection of "permissive" society and a return to the Prophet's presumed way of life. It is currently enjoying great success in France and Europe. The Salafists have a literalist interpretation of the Quran, applying with rigorism a religious vision that owes a great deal to Wahhabism, as practiced in Saudi Arabia. They reject the mingling of men and women, modern gender egalitarianism, and secularism. They practice a quasi-sectarian form of Islam: marriage by preference between members of the group (as in Tablighi Jamaat), identification by mode of dress (beards, jellabas, and qamises for the men, niqabs or burqas for the women).

Do these forms of Islamic fundamentalism encourage the transition to radical Islam? The unequivocal answer is that, on the contrary, in the overwhelming majority of cases such beliefs are a barrier to radicalization. But a problem arises when a few (a tiny minority) pass through these organizations on their way to much more violent religious groups or to self-radicalization. In such cases, it can be presumed that fundamentalism was something like an apprenticeship in a closed vision of Islam, which subsequently took root as violent tendencies. For fragile individuals, membership in these organizations can serve as a rudimentary course of study leading to the violent version of religion. But that is a subjective perception on the individual's part and not the stated aim or explicit intention of the organization.

Religious fundamentalism can desocialize individuals. For example, in embracing Salafism, fundamentalists refuse to mingle with society. They spurn tolerance (perceived as weak and perverted) for other religions, for promiscuity or sexual freedom (which they now see as a sin), and for various forms of consumerism, especially the consumption of alcohol—in short, any attitude deviating from the narrow framework that their religious views dictate. Fundamentalism teaches intolerance, leading believers to deny all legitimacy to other beliefs and behavior. So long as that intolerance remains within the framework of a normative view that does not entail violent acts against others, Salafism can be compared to other forms of sectarianism, which secular citizens perceive as illegitimate but not illegal.

At present, the difference between Islam and other monotheistic religions is that this intolerance more often mutates into violent acts, legitimized by a very marginal but not discredited version of the religion of Allah: jihadism. That transition to violence occurs only very rarely, but a few followers of Tablighi Jamaat or Salafism may have embraced Islamist radicalism after leaving one of these organizations.

The problem is that, in unduly extending suspicion to all followers of Islamic fundamentalism, society stigmatizes them and may thereby contribute to precisely the radicalization it wished to avoid, a sort of self-fulfilling prophecy. This phenomenon sheds light on what is specific to France with respect to radicalization: a "fundamentalist" version of secularity could propel toward radicalization those who might otherwise have confined themselves to a sectarian fundamentalism.

When the fixation on the Islamic veil by a portion of French society and the number of laws and regulations implemented to fight that distinguishing mark of religiosity are taken into account, it becomes clear how generalized suspicion can come to weigh on Islamic fundamentalism, and how that stigma can lead some believers toward an attitude of radical intransigence. The law banning conspicuous religious signs in the schools in 2004, then the outlawing of the burqa in 2010, and the debates raised by the wearing of the Islamic veil in child-care facilities (the Baby-Loup day-care case, in which an employee who wore the Islamic headscarf was dismissed and the decision was contested in court) all reveal a focus, which some call Islamophobic, on the religion of Allah. That makes both devout and nonobservant Muslims ill at ease. There is good reason to speak of a "secular fundamentalism" in France facing off against Islamic fundamentalism, given the skittishness certain secular groups display on the matter of Islamic dress and, more generally, of Islam in the public space.

Nonetheless, jihadist radicalization, though it may attempt to justify itself by citing intolerance of Islam, would exist even in the absence of secular fundamentalism. The horizon of its grievances is much broader than the Islamic headscarf affair: Islamist intolerance drinks deep from the well of extremist ideology characteristic of a new transnational social group that embraces holy war against the entire world. The question of Islamic fundamentalism arises in a French society where national identity, fundamentally political in nature, has been hobbled by economic globalization but also by the denial of national autonomy in a Europe much closer to the multiculturalism of the English-speaking world than to French-style secularism.

SALAFISM: AN EMERGING FORM OF
SECTARIANISM IN ISLAM

About fifteen years ago, Tablighi Jamaat was enjoying great success in the *banlieues*. At present, the Salafists are supplanting them. Their decentralized and flexible mode of organization, their defense of the Wahhabist version of Islam, their conspicuous manner of dress, their vision of the world based on strict segregation of men and women, and their rejection of any compromise with modern ideals make them the partisans par excellence of the rigorist version of Islam. They reject that description, saying they are simply defending *authentic* Islam, the others being inauthentic by definition. Wherever they find themselves, they join together in solidarity; their cohesion is locally strong, for their manner of dress allows their followers to recognize one another easily. In the *banlieues* as in prison, most conversions conform to their model of religiosity. The Salafists embody an Islamic ideal resting on two principles: an inflexibility grounded in the "Text" (*nass*, in other words, the Quran) and a reading that excludes from the Quran and the Hadith any conciliatory view of tolerance and openness toward the diversity of religious conceptions. Salafism fulfills a basic counter-anomic function, providing simple, imaginary solutions to the real and complex problems of modernity, and puts an end to feelings of solitude and the loss of guideposts from which its followers suffered. It imposes limits where modern boundaries remain vague. It clearly distinguishes between the rights of men and of women (in contradistinction to modern egalitarianism) and between the permitted and the prohibited. In the modern anomic world, anything that does not harm others is supposedly allowed, which opens possibilities but also subjects individuals to the arduous task of dealing with their freedom. Salafism clearly divides the righteous from the unrighteous, what lies within the realm of human beings and their free will from what belongs to God and His omnipotence. The religious becomes omnipresent and encloses in its net many areas that modern societies allocate to individual free will or collective suffrage.[15]

In the Salafist conception, Islam is presented as the antidote to laxity and to the modern powerlessness to govern one's life without falling into despair and nihilism. Obviously, a number of sympathizers embrace Salafism only for a time, then drift away because of its rigorism. But a hard core has constituted itself and has now taken root in a national and even local "tradition": the movement can boast of a second generation that is following the path of the first, having learned Arabic along the way. They give readings of the Quran, spelling out the permitted and the prohibited independently of the imams in other branches of Islam (such as those at the Mosque of Paris), and gradually take possession of new places of worship as the movement spreads in the big cities and *banlieues* (see Adraoui 2013). The great majority of those who embrace the main current of Salafism in the outlying neighborhoods keep their distance from jihadism. Their primary aim is Islamization from below, and they dream not of jihad but of *hijra*, "exodus" to Islamic lands where they could live their faith more freely than they do in secular France. But a few followers do not find that version of faith earnest enough and opt for an extremist view that favors armed struggle.

The Salafists are now part of the Muslim landscape in France, and a few of their believers can be found in all the big cities; in several they already have their own mosque. Most of the converts are attracted by the Salafists' rigorist version of Islam, which in fact appears the most legitimate to many Muslims, even those who do not follow it strictly. Within about a decade, they have succeeded in constituting an intelligentsia that decrees what is licit and illicit. Followers zealously learn Arabic and study the Quran and Hadith, which, on a wide range of subjects, corroborate their point of view about other, more moderate versions of Islam (such as Muslim reformism).

Some Salafists, though inflexible on the matter of faith, make their peace with a number of infringements of the law, such as the trafficking in illicit goods (drugs), which might seem to be incompatible with religious orthodoxy. They justify themselves by invoking the necessities of life in a society of *jahiliyya*, where faith in Allah does not reign and where Islamic values are not respected.

The great majority of Salafists espouse a rigorist fundamentalism whose closed horizons reflect a sectarian but nonviolent religiosity rather than the will to fight society through violence. Nevertheless, that religious conception is a departure from the dominant forms of Islam and introduces a mode of being that risks desocializing those who embrace it. In any event, Salafism constitutes a challenge to current secular norms, but in the name of fundamentalism, not jihadism.

RADICALIZATION IN PRISON

Radicalization does not occur solely in the larger society: it can also take place within organizations and institutions such as prisons, the army, the schools, even hospitals.

No phenomenon of mass radicalization has as yet been observed in schools, hospitals, or the regular army. Prison remains the most vulnerable institution. Individuals who have been convicted or are awaiting trial, often suffering from a strained relationship with society and sometimes from social frustration, economic exclusion, or cultural stigmatization, are forced to live together. For them, institutional constraints may find expression in a greater receptiveness to radicalization.

Radicalization in prison challenges the validity of "rational choice" theory, at least with respect to a large portion of those I call the radicalized, as opposed to the radicalizers. Radicalizers play on the psychological fragility of the individuals they intend to lead toward extremism, while seeking to evade the attention of the intelligence services. That is why they opt for very small groups (two or three members in all).

I have learned a great deal about that new model by observing one particular case in prison. A very mentally fragile young man (broken family, violence, problems adapting to life after leaving his parents' home) is serving a sentence of more than ten years, without the possibility of early release, for an aggravated offense. The judge failed to believe his claim that the crime was not premeditated. The prisoner was approached by a radical Islamist, who succeeded in gaining power over his fragile psyche and indoctrinating him with a focus on holy war. By the time those in charge of the prison belatedly realized the radicalizer's influence and had him transferred to another facility, the task of radicalization was already complete. After that separation, the radicalized man's condition deteriorated.

The radicalizer had cast a spell: he exerted a particular type of enchantment over the prisoner, who became fascinated by the extremist view of things, unable to exercise his critical faculties or to inform himself personally about the ideology or vision in question. (Most radicalized individuals are not under a spell; they have an ideology that they embrace of their own free will.) So long as the radicalizer supported the indoctrination with his presence, the fragile prisoner fared well; he showed signs of improvement in his behavior and seemed to thrive for a short time. That phenomenon can be compared to the manic phase in those suffering from bipolar disorder. But once the radicalizer was removed by the prison authorities, the radicalized individual fell into a profound depression, much more severe than in the past. The spell cast was exerting its devastating effects on his behavior in multiple forms (withdrawal, suicidal tendencies, instigation of fights, and delusions about jihad). That pattern can be found in several pairs of individuals who underwent radicalization in a vacuum, with various nuances depending on the radicalized's degree of lucidity.

This new type of radicalization calls into question the psychological normality of a significant portion of the people involved, whether radicalized or radicalizers. And yet, in the dominant theories, normality is postulated for the majority of such subjects.[16] In prison, a number of psychologically fragile—even psychopathic and unstable—individuals are fascinated by radicalization. They easily manage to join very small groups, given that it has become impossible to constitute organized groups in which instrumental rationality would gain the upper hand. In organizations such as al-Qaeda before September 11, the need for effectiveness excluded people who were mentally too fragile. In the new paradigm, both charismatic leaders (radicalizers) and the radicalized are vulnerable to mental problems.

Islam is the focal point for a number of prisoners because, in Europe, it has become "the religion of the oppressed." It attracts young people belonging to the second or third generation of the Maghrebi immigration, who suffer from anomie and are victims of racism. Young converts find in radical Islam the anti-imperialist dimension that in the 1970s was incarnated by radical leftist movements. At least as regards their violent elements, these movements have now left the scene. Embracing Islam can thus assume a multiplicity of meanings, from the desire to cross swords with an arrogant West (anti-imperialism) to the wish to return to a patriarchal family, in which the roles of women and men are defined inequitably. For the relatively few young women who embrace Islam, a paradoxical self-affirmation is at play, one at odds with Western cultural orientations. These women choose a patriarchalism that rejects feminism and its achievements over the past half century.

Prison is the crucible where the identity crises of the children and grandchildren of North African immigrants find a privileged site for development, if only because of the high proportion of this group within the prison population. Most likely, about half of all prisoners are Muslims, whereas Muslims, observant or not, constitute only about 8 percent of the French population.[17]

Radicalization in prison reflects some of the major trends at work in French society, but prison space is also unique: control by the authorities is much greater than on the outside, but because of overcrowding, radicalization can intensify in unprecedented ways. Nor should television be overlooked. A few years ago, access to television was relatively expensive, but at present, various public channels are available for less than 10 euros a month. Television now plays a leading role in the socialization of prisoners in general and specifically in the exacerbation of their sense of injustice concerning the Muslim world, its unrest, and the way the West works out problems by intervening directly or indirectly.

It is interesting to compare the reactions of Muslim prisoners to the Merah case. According to most of those interviewed, Merah should not have attacked children, not even Jewish ones; though a few interpreted his actions as inspired by Islam, others saw only impulsiveness and blind hatred. Most important, however, a number of prisoners concealed their real viewpoint, evading the issue in one way or another, for fear that I was an informer for the police or the prison authorities. It was other, sometimes older prisoners who, speaking more freely, communicated to me the admiration that some of the young prisoners felt for Merah, despite his murder of children, of which most of them disapproved. Mohamed Merah has been something of a contested hero for some young people in the *banlieues* and prisons in the present decade, just as Khaled Kelkal was some fifteen years ago—both were shot dead by the police, and their death elevated them to the rank of hero for some, religious martyr for others.

Radicalization in prison is also related to living conditions. The overall organization of the prison, even its architecture, can favor or stand in the way of radicalization. In some prisons, such as the

national penitentiary of Clairvaux, a tradition of "liberal" management and tolerance limits the everyday frustration of prison life and,
as a result, the radicalization to which it can lead. Conversely, a
steady succession of humiliations and the incomprehension the authorities show toward legitimate demands of prisoners—access to
recreation, especially sports; a decent life in a cell with a maximum
of two occupants; normal conditions for exercising one's faith (collective Friday prayer for Muslims); and less draconian conditions
for seeing family in the visiting room—cannot fail to have consequences. Harsh discipline contributes to radicalization.

FRUSTRATION IN PRISON

For many reasons, including the limited number of Muslim chaplains, Muslims are unable to celebrate collective prayer on Friday in
many prisons. That gives rise to deep frustrations among prisoners,
observant or not, who experience that impossibility as a demonstration of contempt for Islam on the part of the institution. It makes little
difference whether that feeling is well founded (it is in part, especially
where the staff's attitude is concerned, but many grievances prisoners formulate against the institution's rejection of Islam can be
attributed to causes other than Islamophobia). A number of prisoners,
rightly or wrongly, sincerely think that Islam is a target of discrimination when compared to Christianity and Judaism. They readily
cite restrictions associated with the exercise of the Muslim religion in
prison, in particular, the absence of collective Friday prayer, whereas
Sabbath prayers for Jews and Sunday services for Christians are
offered as a matter of course.

Adding to that major frustration:

- The difficulty of bringing into the prison a prayer rug,
  often prohibited by the prison authorities, who see it as a
  more or less conspicuous sign of religiosity in the public

space. Prisoners, by contrast, consider it an integral part of their individual practice of prayer, but also of their collective practice, since most of the worship halls in prisons lack a large rug. Some prayer rugs, however, incorporate a metal compass to indicate the direction of Mecca and therefore cannot pass through the security checks, because the compass might not be the only metal object in the rug, and it would have to be torn in several places to ensure that that is not the case.

- The ban on wearing jellabas and qamises, considered by the administration of most prisons to be a conspicuous sign of religiosity.

- The difficulty in obtaining halal meat or other ingredients in the dining halls of certain prisons. Prisoners sometimes call the available brands of halal chicken and red meat fraudulent and attribute to the prison the deliberate intention of deceiving them. They often evoke as support for their views televised broadcasts denouncing brands that have been "tampered with."

- The shortage of imams with whom to share concerns and complaints. Like priests for Catholics, imams have the important function of being confidants of a sort for prisoners, who would like to communicate their worries and anxieties and find a religiously authorized response to them. Often, however, to have access to an imam, they must write to him and wait several weeks before a first visit is scheduled, assuming it ever takes place. These waiting periods are long and difficult to bear for prisoners who feel the need to talk to a trustworthy person.

- The inadequacy of the food rations offered to prisoners to mark the breaking of the fast in the evenings during Ramadan. The packet, containing milk, dates, fruit juice, and a few other ingredients, seems to provoke anger or bitter irony from prisoners, who see it as an obvious mark of contempt by prison authorities for their religion and their person. Given the meagerness of that packet, Christmas parcels become a problem: Why not allow the same type of parcels for Muslim holidays? prisoners asked. For them, the choice of Christmas clearly showed the supremacy of Christianity in what is supposed to be a secular republic.

In prison, Islam is generally experienced by a portion of its followers as a religion consigned to inferior status; they are "internally oppressed." The sense of victimhood is highly developed among Muslims in prison and can easily translate into the language of generalized frustration.

MUSLIM CHAPLAINS AND THEIR
DIFFICULT ROLE AS MEDIATORS

In less than a decade, the number of Muslim chaplains serving French prisons has more than doubled, from about 60 before 2005 to about 160 at present. But that statistic conceals a serious shortfall. If we assume that half of all prisoners are Muslim (for legal reasons, there are no statistics, but that figure, which includes the observant and the nonobservant, was supported by officials in my interviews), at least three times the current number of imams would be needed to satisfy the demands of prisoners for the same conditions enjoyed by Catholics and Protestants.

The inadequate number of imams is obvious in detention facilities, especially those near big cities, and the high demand from prisoners cannot be satisfied under current conditions. That low number favors radicalizers who proclaim themselves imams and propose their radical vision to some of the prisoners. They thus transform into holy wrath the hatred that some, especially those of North African descent, already bear toward society. And once hatred is transcribed into the register of the sacred, a profound change occurs. Such hatred attacks the social body in blind fury and may be expressed as generalized murder. That change is incomparably more dangerous than the atomized deviance or delinquency that motivates individuals seeking to enrich themselves and rise to the level of the middle classes, from which they feel wrongfully excluded by ill will and racism. Without a member of the clergy to prevent the sacralization of hatred, unstable persons who have known only exclusion and a feeling of worthlessness may translate their rage and desire for vengeance into this totalizing form, becoming jihadists. They do so by appealing to the mythified past of their Muslim ancestors, whose ghosts haunt them as the only reference point for an authenticity from which they feel barred. Prison can thus become a formidable place where young outcasts from Muslim backgrounds discover a martial Islam, where it takes only a few fanatics to turn them into hawks acting in the name of holy war.

In any case, some young people undergoing radicalization avoid the imams, whom they see as henchmen of the penitentiary administration. Or they think the imams are incompetent—or less competent than they—in interpreting the teachings of Islam. Some prisoners vie with one another in their Islamic erudition, especially their knowledge of Islamic law (*fiqh*) and the reading and recitation of the Quran, governed by the rules of *tajwid* ("elocution," the precise pronunciation of ancient Arabic), a difficult art that requires hundreds of additional hours of study. For them, prison becomes the place for a more thorough understanding of Islamic laws and precepts, which may turn them away from radicalization. They then think about immigrating to Islamic regions after release from prison, rather than engaging in holy war. To jihad (holy war), they prefer *hijra* (exodus), a peaceful solution to a conflict in identity or a religious vision at odds with secularized society. As a result, their relation to Muslim chaplains becomes neutral.

On the whole, imams play a fairly positive role in the lives of prisoners, more of whom might become radicalized in their absence. They appeal to Quranic notions at the opposite extreme from those elaborated by religious extremists. For example, an imam for a large Île-de-France prison devoted several discussion sessions to the notion of patience (*sabr*), emphasizing the need not to rush into risky ventures but to summon patience for the better times promised by God.

PRISON RADICALIZATION AND ITS SUBJECTS

Of all the institutions where radicalization can develop, prison occupies a place apart. Many cases of radicalization have been observed there, either under the influence of individuals already convicted of "criminal conspiracy for the purpose of committing terrorist offenses" or more or less autonomously, in the name of an extremist ideology. The frustration caused by prison life is often a contributing factor.

Three categories of radicalized prisoners can be distinguished:

- Those with an extensive history of terrorist offenses and criminal convictions.
- Those seeking a protector from gang leaders or others seeking to exploit their moral or physical weakness. Their radicalization is instrumental, at least at first. Subsequently, the mechanisms of action and the group dynamic can turn them into authentic jihadists.
- Those who set out to capitalize on their membership in the Islamist movement to acquire more prestige or a greater freedom to act. For them, radical Islamism is a springboard to achieving "glory," especially in prison. Although their motivations differ from those in the first group, they take their place alongside the convicted terrorists, or they self-radicalize in actuality.

This last group is somewhat on the decline because of actions taken by prison administrators, such as close, daily surveillance of those found guilty of terrorism or proselytism and of those suspected of owing their prestige among other prisoners to their allegiance to radical Islam. But something of that group remains, for example, in the popularity among some young people of Mohamed Merah's imprisoned brother. Abdelkader Merah is considered the brother of a hero, the heroism of his younger sibling reflecting favorably on him, especially because his incarceration proves that he shares his brother's views and may even have assisted him. For prisoners who suffer from being "less than zero," it is important to find a way to distinguish themselves from the crowd and achieve "glory."

The role of the already radicalized is essential. They may translate the political into the religious for prisoners who, before meeting them, did not speak the idiom of Islamic exceptionalism. These already radicalized prisoners embody the politicization of Islam: the religious becomes an ideology of combat in the name of a political conception of the sacred. The already radicalized may be charismatic personalities, leaders who can give meaning to the frustration of psychologically fragile prisoners looking for a scapegoat (France, the West, or a particular country), translating their malaise into a redemptive act.

Radical Islamists encourage prisoners to consider Islam less like an individual and ritualistic mode of life and more like a collective diktat. They lead prisoners to adopt a vision in which the political is a subcategory of the religious. Already radicalized prisoners can easily "translate" political grievances into religious imperatives. Every political and social event is then interpreted in terms of radicalized Islam, and the miracle solution is recourse to sacralized violence.

9

The New Radicalism on the March

Radicalization takes place in an international environment marked by the emergence of the Muslim world as a theater for Islamist and even jihadist movements, beginning with the Islamic Revolution in Iran in 1979. The 1990s–2010s saw a change in strategy by radical Islamist movements such as al-Qaeda—displacement of the target from the "enemy near at hand," the Muslim regimes, to the "remote enemy," the United States and Europe (Filiu 2006). With the Arab Spring of 2010–2011, the Muslim world experienced a temporary respite from radical Islamism, which resumed with even greater force upon the failure of states in Libya and Yemen, and especially because of the civil war in Syria, which has attracted young people undergoing radicalization throughout the world, notably Europe, and in particular, France.[1]

Since the 1980s, jihadism has been through several phases in many countries, beginning with Afghanistan, where the Soviet invasion in 1979 opened a front to which Islamists, aided by the West, rushed from all sides to fight the Soviet regime. The historical origins of al-Qaeda date to that period, when bin Laden and his assistants sent volunteers trained in segregated camps to Afghanistan. In 1989, once the war was over and the Russian army had left, a large portion of these "Afghans" (veterans of Afghanistan, so named by their native countries) returned home, this time to launch domestic jihad. They trained the first jihadist cells in the various societies, teaching techniques of guerrilla warfare and bomb making, even though, in the low-intensity conflict of the Afghanistan war, foreign jihadists had often been left out of the battles.

Subsequently, a new generation of jihadists emerged, in the West and in the Muslim world, composed of young people whose war training had taken place on the Web much more than on the ground. On the whole, they have proved to be mediocre fabricators of incendiary devices but discerning connoisseurs of the Internet and its arcana.

It is now possible to speak of a third generation of jihadists, whose training is taking place in those Arab countries with failed states, following the crisis brought on by the Arab Spring, especially in Yemen, Libya, and along the Algeria-Tunisia border, but also and above all in Syria. That country has been in the grip of a terrible civil war since 2013. (In 2012, there was still a peaceful opposition, which attempted to maintain the ideals of the Arab Spring despite the intensification of street fighting.) There is now a triangular front: Assad's army faces off against the Free Syrian Army but also against jihadists (al-Nusra Front and other groups that embrace radical Islam, such as ISIS, also known as the Islamic State). Fighting also occurs between rival jihadist groups, al-Nusra and ISIS.

More than ten thousand foreign jihadists are waging war in Syria, approximately two thousand of them Europeans and about a thousand Tunisians.[2] They find themselves thrust into the heart of violent battles. In Afghanistan, there were three thousand to five thousand foreign jihadists, only 10 percent of whom took part in battles, the rest remaining in the camps or in Pakistani tribal zones (Bergen 2006); probably about fifty Arabs from the Middle East perished, versus a million Afghans, and foreign combatants represented less than 0.5 percent of the forces fighting the Soviets.[3]

That state of affairs stands in contrast to the situation in Syria. In the first place, it is no longer possible, as it was in Afghanistan, to remain in low-intensity conflict zones. Second, the proportion of foreign to domestic jihadists has profoundly changed. It is likely that the Free Syrian Army has no more than about a hundred thousand combatants (its regular troops are estimated at eighty thousand, fifty to sixty thousand of them at the front),[4] so the ten thousand or so foreign jihadists constitute roughly 10 percent of the fighters, far more than the percentage of foreign radical Islamists among the Afghani forces.

Several of these young people have already met their death in Syria, such as the French half brothers Jean-Daniel and Nicolas Bons (nicknamed Abu Abd al Rahman), the first in August 2013, the second in December of the same year; and the British Choukri Ellekhlifi, of Moroccan descent, nicknamed Abu Hujama al-Britani, who was killed in August 2013, having previously attempted to finance his jihad by theft, threatening several people in the streets of London.

Fundraising for jihadists in Syria is said to occur in Great Britain, but also in France and in Muslim countries such as Saudi Arabia, Qatar, and the United Arab Emirates. As already noted, before they leave and even at the beginning of their stay in Syria, European jihadists often speak of a "humanitarian mission" in their interviews or messages, thus perpetuating a tradition that in France originated with the famous Roubaix gang, active in 1996. Some members of that group—Lionel Dumont, for example—participated in humanitarian missions in Croatia before joining the radical Islamists in the war in Bosnia. Aspiring European jihadists come to identify with the jihadist group through the brotherhood of arms, as their immersion in battles alongside hardened jihadists proceeds. At first, they share the low-level tasks (handing out water, cooking, transporting the wounded, and so on) to which new arrivals are assigned and also undergo more or less rudimentary training and ideological indoctrination. Because they do not speak Arabic, European jihadists are often grouped together by native country. The bonds of affection created between individuals of the same nationality can be invaluable for setting up an extremist group in their native country once they have returned.

According to relatively reliable sources, practically no country in western Europe is free from jihadist recruitment. Take the example of Burak Karan, a young German soccer player of Turkish descent who seemed to have a brilliant future as a professional; some of his fellow athletes, such as Sami Khedira, Dennis Aogo, and Kevin-Prince Boateng, also children of immigration, became stars. But Karan died in Syria in October 2013, near the city of Azaz, killed in an air strike by the Assad regime.[5]

Danish jihadists are not to be outdone. Abu Khattab, very likely killed on the Syrian front in November 2013, uploaded two videos to YouTube, in which he advocated jihad in Danish. According to Khattab, the softness of Danish life is only a snare, intended to lead young Muslims away from the path of jihad: "We were provided with everything in Denmark. Our parents paid for everything, we were given free bread and milk, but the [infidels] could not fool us. . . . My dear brothers, jihad is the greatest reward. Your blood will smell sweet . . . my dear brothers and sisters in Denmark, you should come too. It's the best thing to do to strengthen the Muslim people and the Islamic State."

Danish jihadists also include Abderrozak Benarabe, leader of the Blågårds Plads gang, who joined Ahrar al-Sham, a radical group in Syria. In 2006 he was charged with having bribed two Poles to execute five people in Denmark. Acquitted in 2010, he was later convicted of assault and blackmail. Benarabe's gang participated in a gang war in Copenhagen between biker groups and immigrant groups. Some of its members met again in Syria alongside the jihadists. According to another video, Shiraz Tariq, leader of the Salafist group Kaldet til Islam (Called to Islam), met holy death in Syria in the very radical Jaish al-Muhajireen wal-Ansar (Army of Migrants and Companions of the Prophet), in which several thousand foreign jihadists fight the Syrian army with the ultimate aim of martyrdom.[6] Another Danish jihadist, Slimane Hadj Abderrahmane, a former prisoner at Guantanamo, is said to have been killed in Syria in early 2013, fighting in the jihadist al-Nusra Front. He had been arrested in Afghanistan in 2001 and transferred to Guantanamo, and was then released in 2004. In 2007 he served ten months in prison for stealing credit cards.

These examples point to a lost generation almost everywhere in Europe, part of whom had been involved in delinquent behavior and sought to give meaning to their lives through the adventure of jihadism, moving among different countries and finding their life's purpose in their absolute engagement, a contrast from their criminal past. The search for meaning, in this case, entails a revolt against society and the assertion of a self that breaks its moorings from the surrounding world and often from family, in the name of a heroic holy war. Society is hated all the more for treating as inferior this generation descended from Muslim working-class immigrants. That phenomenon affects the United States to a much lesser degree (it is estimated that about a hundred Americans have gone to Syria to wage jihad), even though many Muslims believe that U.S. policy is much more repressive in their regard than European. This predominantly European character of the new jihadism can be explained by the proximity of the Middle East and by the precarious or excluded status of young people from Muslim backgrounds in Europe, which fuels their identity crisis and victimhood. In the United States, by contrast, white Muslims tend to belong to the middle and upper middle classes.

It should be noted that many jihadists in Syria come from the Arab world, especially Egypt, the United Arab Emirates, and Libya, which also supplies arms (Gaddafi's arsenals fell into the hands of warlords, who sell them to the highest bidder).

Foreign jihadists in Syria are between about fifteen and thirty years old. A portion of these jihadists will survive the war and return to Europe (especially France); in fact, that movement has already begun. Even if the intelligence services manage to identify the great majority of them, they will certainly not be able to monitor them all or assemble enough evidence to send them to prison. Europe has already experienced several attacks committed by individuals whom the intelligence services had identified but let go for lack of evidence or because no one could predict how dangerous they were. Mohamed Merah had been under surveillance, and Michael Adebolajo and Michael Adebowale were known to be radical Islamists, but that is not enough to arrest someone in a democracy.

Of the jihadists who survive Syria, some North African nationals will come to Europe, especially France, because of their family ties to the Maghrebi diaspora. New antiterrorist systems should be set in place, entailing not only repression but also persuasion and the integration of individuals—in particular, procedures of deradicalization that connect members of the jihadists' home neighborhoods with municipal authorities and religious bodies, as well as the police and psychiatrists.

10

Radicalization Versus Deradicalization

To prevent radicalization, many European countries have set in place so-called deradicalization procedures, a type of intervention intended to return those who have engaged in jihadism to "normality," defined as the renunciation of violence as a solution to the evils from which society suffers. In some democracies, such as the United States, that will to neutralize the radicalized sometimes overrode respect for human rights (arbitrary arrest without trial, as at Guantanamo; torture, such as waterboarding, and other unacceptable forms of psychological or physical pressure, at Abu Ghraib Prison during the U.S. Army's occupation of Iraq). In nondemocratic countries, like most of the countries in the Middle East and North Africa, the notion of official deradicalization programs is even more problematic. How can we trust governments that repress the population in defiance of popular will? How can we have faith that they are not mistreating detainees? And how can we believe their deradicalization statistics? Saudi Arabia, for example, boasts a success rate of more than 90 percent for its deradicalization program. That figure has little merit, given the substance of the programs and their sociopolitical aims, as well as the enormous benefits granted. The "deradicalized" are offered fairly well-paid employment, material and financial encouragement to marry, and ideological supervision to divert them from their vision of radical Islam and lead them to adopt a "moderate" doctrine.

In any event, deradicalization in a democracy must proceed with respect for personal conscience and then implement procedures leading those convicted of terrorism-related offenses to no longer consider violence a privileged mode of action. Obviously, deradicalization, attempted in Great Britain and, under its direct inspiration, the United States, as well as in a few European countries, such as Norway (for neo-Nazis), can serve directly or indirectly as a model for modes of intervention by the public authorities in other European societies. That influence can be of service to both sides, if it is set in place with the collaboration of the police, municipalities, and neighborhood groups (what are called communities in the English-speaking world, acknowledgment of which is denounced in France as a first step toward communitarianism).

Directives addressed to European countries were devised by the European Commission to implement measures intended to prevent radicalization (European Commission 2014). In France, given the distrust of the public authorities regarding that type of action, in a context where the religious and the political are kept separate, no deradicalization program has as yet come into being, and only one plan to fight networks funneling potential jihadists into Syria has been set in place by the government: the establishment of a toll-free number for families with a child vulnerable to radicalization.[1] Denial of passports, especially to minors, and a system for individualized reintegration are other measures being considered within the framework of that plan.

Conclusion

As information and the economy are globalized, what happens in one corner of the world ultimately has unimagined repercussions elsewhere. The civil war in Syria, the development of jihadism in that country—with the participation of young Europeans and Maghrebis who become ever more radicalized and learn to handle weapons—will have unprecedented consequences in Europe when these young people return. If no solution is devised, their violent acts will increase fear, racism, and Islamophobia.

Radicalization is protean: it innovates and adapts to every new context while attempting to neutralize the struggle of states against it. For the moment, jihadism is the favored expression of the new radicalism, in the West and in the Muslim world. But radicalization can also encompass other ideologies, such as xenophobic and anti-Islamic extremism on the far right and violence in the name of other causes (anti-abortion in the United States, radical environmentalism, and others). In each case, the procedures for action are adjusted to fit the particular circumstances, keeping pace with changes in the intelligence services responsible for combating them.

The new forms of radicalization are more unpredictable but more limited in scope than previous ones. In the West, the individuals involved are fewer, the groups are smaller, the followers are more psychologically fragile, but their capacity for violence is more limited than at the time of the attacks of September 11, 2001, when nearly three thousand met their death through the murderous acts of nineteen radicalized men controlled by al-Qaeda. By virtue of the very success of the intelligence services and law enforcement throughout the West, the destructiveness of a single attack is more limited than it once was in that part of the world, especially in France. On the one hand, the radicalized have become more unpredictable (the police have trouble identifying individuals or very small groups); on the other, they do less damage because the mobilization of policing services now impels them to operate in groups of a few individuals at most.

Radicalization has changed form in the last few decades. The Islamic Revolution in Iran in 1979, the war in Afghanistan beginning with the Soviet invasion the same year, the various complications at the end of the war in 1989, the incubation period for a new type of jihadism against the United States ("the remote enemy"), and the attacks of September 11, 2001, were all critical moments. Subsequently, beginning in the twenty-first century, homegrown jihadism has become the most common type in Europe.[1] The Arab Spring of 2010–2011 inaugurated a new era, which culminated in the civil war in Syria and the collapse of states in Libya and Yemen. We are witnessing a new era of radical Islamism: al-Qaeda, placed on the defensive a few years earlier by the American attacks, is managing to reconstitute itself in a decentralized form, especially in Iraq and Syria, but also in Egypt (in the Sinai Desert) and Tunisia (particularly along the Algerian border). In Syria, the concentration of several thousand jihad fighters, including nearly two thousand Europeans, portends real difficulties when these waves of young people return, if appropriate solutions are not adopted. How can we deal with the several hundred French citizens—but also Belgian, English, German, Danish, and many others—who will come back to

Europe after waging holy war in Syria? Repressive measures will not suffice. We will have to engage in deradicalization in a form adapted to French secularism. We will need to constitute groups composed of imams, municipal leaders, police officers, neighborhood authorities (male elders, called "white beards"), and psychologists to direct confused young people, accustomed to seeing violence as the only possible solution to their problems, toward a different life. We will have to integrate these young people into life in society in a way that encourages them to avoid the vicious cycle of escalating violence followed by prison or death.

France, however, because of the strict religious neutrality of its secular state, is not known for its capacity to promote that type of hybrid structure, which is already in place in the United Kingdom and many other European countries, as well as in the United States. The world's entire repressive arsenal will not be enough to end ideological violence if it is not accompanied by psychological and theological support that can change the faith fighters' view of the world. Rigid secularism would prevent cooperation between religious and civil authorities within flexible institutions grounded in real communities. We will have to overcome that fear of too great a proximity to religion if we are to stop outbreaks of violence.

Jihadism has led to a partial suspension of certain fundamental freedoms, of expression especially, by creating situations that impelled lawmakers increasingly to assimilate extremist propaganda to acts subject to legal punishment. The provisions regarding "media jihad" (or incitement to violence in Great Britain) are thus akin to a legal recognition of "intent crimes." That modification of the law, set in place in conformance with public opinion, blurs the boundary between speech and deed. Speech is now considered a "speech act" rather than a verbal expression whose freedom is guaranteed by democracy. If these restrictions on freedom of expression last a few more decades, they will seem normal to the following generations, thus limiting freedom of speech, which was a matter of course for the founders of democracy.

More broadly, the new forms of extremism—jihadism being the predominant form for more than a decade—are indicators of a profound malaise in the contemporary world. They may, of course, be chalked up to individual responsibility or religious or ideological radicalism. But the malaise of modern societies—which Durkheim viewed as a relaxation of the social bond—combined with economic exclusion within a mass culture that is egalitarian by its very essence, gives rise to a new malady over which our societies have only imperfect control. Globalization has gone hand in hand with a profound feeling of oppression and frustration, which is no longer kept in check by ideologies, as it was during the Cold War. If citizenship is defined as economic and social integration into a society, then the affliction of some while others prosper in a globalized world devoid of true global citizenship will continue to haunt all citizens in the form of radicalized terrorism.

NOTES

Introduction: The Notion of Radicalization

1. I use the word *terrorist* in an almost journalistic sense, knowing full well that someone called a terrorist by one side is perceived as a resistance fighter or liberator on the other.

2. In the past decade the number of people killed by radical Islamists has been much higher in the Muslim world than in the West.

3. Historically, *terrorism*—a relatively old term, dating to 1794—signified the doctrine of the Reign of Terror. Terrorism was an exercise of power by the state, not in opposition to it. The advocates of the Reign of Terror, led by Robespierre, exercised power from March 1793 to July 1794. The struggle against the state under the ancien régime and violence against the authorities were covered by the notion of tyrannicide. It was only in the nineteenth century that *terrorism* came to designate the struggle against power and the state through violence.

4. See Farhad Khosrokhavar (2009 and 2011). An exhaustive bibliography is provided at the end of those books.

5. For a summary of the different theories of radicalization, with reference to radical Islamism in particular, see Khosrokhavar (2009, chap. 1, "Explanatory Approaches to Jihadism").

6. See Donatella Della Porta, "Research Design and Methodological Considerations," in *Patterns of Radicalization in Political Activism: Research Design*, ed. Donatella Della Porta and Claudius Wagemann, Veto Project Report (Florence: European University Institute, 2005).

7. See McCauley and Moskalenko (2011). In this work, the authors study the paths that lead to radicalization by focusing on the individual or collective grievances of the radicalized within the reference group; they analyze the "slippery slope," that is, the gradual radicalization of members of the group as their individual freedom is reduced and as heroism, sacrifice, danger, and the love of risk are valorized, favoring the most adventurous and procuring them high status within the group. The values of the closed group gain the upper hand over those of society and become the frame of reference for the group's members.

8. See Ami Pedahzur (2004), who has proposed a three-stage model.

9. In the fantasies of the far right, "Eurabia" designates an Arabized Europe.

10. "Pakis" are English citizens of Pakistani descent living in poor neighborhoods in the big cities of Great Britain.

1: The History of Radicalization

1. In France, Adolphe Thiers ordered the massacre of thirty thousand Communards in 1871; and in Chicago on May 4, 1886, in what is known as the Haymarket massacre, police opened fire at a labor demonstration, killing about thirty, in reprisal for a bombing.

2: Islamist Radicalization in the Muslim World

1. *Hittisme*: an Algerian neologism meaning to do nothing for hours on end, leaning against a wall and forming groups that spend part of the night that way.

2. *Trabendisme*: a term for illegal trafficking in Algeria, which also applies perfectly to the situation in the French *banlieues*.

3. See International Organization for Migration, World Migration Report 2010, www.iom.int/world-migration-report-2010 (consulted in June 2016).

4. Before the Americans overthrew the Taliban in 2002–2003, al-Qaeda and other Sunni jihadist groups benefited from the hospitality offered by the authorities in Afghanistan. Since then, no state officially harbors Sunni jihadists.

5. Guy Taillefer, "Portrait-robot de la femme kamikaze: Qui est-elle et pourquoi le fait-elle?" *Le Devoir*, Nov. 25, 2005, www.ledevoir.com/societe/actualites -en-societe/96139/portrait-robot-de-la-femme-kamikaze (consulted in June 2016).

3: The Jihadist Intelligentsia and Its Globalization

1. Shane Scott and Souad Mekhennet, "Imam's Path from Condemning Terror to Preaching Jihad," *New York Times*, May 8, 2010, www.nytimes.com/2010/05 /09/world/09awlaki.html (last consulted in June 2016).

4: The Web

1. See the report by Ghaffar Hussain and Erin Marie Saltman, *Jihad Trending: A Comprehensive Analysis of Online Extremism and How to Counter It* (Quilliam, 2014), www.quilliamfoundation.org.

2. See Bill Roggio, "Syria's Jihadist Twitter Wars," *Daily Beast*, Feb. 16, 2014.

3. "La lutte contre le 'djihad médiatique' franchit un cap," *Le Point*, Sept. 20, 2013, www.lepoint.fr/societe/la-lutte-contre-le-djihad-mediatique-franchit-un-cap -20-09-2013-1733508_23.php (last consulted in June 2016).

4. The magazine *Inspire* is regularly named in antiterrorist legal proceedings, especially in France: it was read by a young woman questioned in October 2013 in the Belleville neighborhood of Paris for having attempted to make contact with the organization al-Qaeda in the Arabian Peninsula (AQAP); she was caught at the home of members of the so-called Cannes-Torcy cell, which was dismantled in 2012. It was also in the pages of *Inspire* that the Tsarnaev brothers, who perpetrated the double attacks at the Boston Marathon on April 15, 2013, learned how to make their bombs. See Jean-Noël Mirande, "Paris: Une femme soupçonnée de liens

avec al-Qaida arrêtée," *Le Point*, Oct. 1, 2013, http://www.lepoint.fr/societe/paris
-une-femme-soupconnee-de-liens-avec-al-qaida-arretee-01-10-2013-1737093_23
.php (last consulted in June 2016).

5. "France: Le cyber-jihadiste Romain Letellier, alias Abou Siyad al-Normandy,
condamné à un an de prison ferme," www.rfi.fr/france/20140305-cyber-jihadiste
-francais-condamne-prison-ferme-terrorisme-letellier-abou-siyad-al-normandy
-guerre-sainte, published Mar. 4, 2014 (consulted in June 2016).

5: Financing Radicalization

1. Zarate (2013); Joby Warrick and Tik Root, "Islamic Charity Officials Gave
Millions to al-Qaeda, U.S. Says," *Washington Post*, Dec. 23, 2013, https://www.wash
ingtonpost.com/world/national-security/islamic-charity-officials-gave-millions-to
-al-qaeda-us-says/2013/12/22/e0c53ad6-69b8-11e3-a0b9-249bbb34602c_story
.html (last consulted in June 2016).

6: Sites of Radicalization

1. Claire Ané, "Avant Merah, peu d'islamistes avaient grandi et frappé en
France," *Le Monde*, Mar. 29, 2012, www.lemonde.fr/societe/article/2012/03/29
/avant-merah-peu-d-islamistes-avaient-grandi-et-frappe-en-france_1676550_3224
.html (last consulted in June 2016).

2. Jonathan Githens-Mazer, "Why Woolwich Matters: The South London
Angle," *RUSI Analysis*, Royal United Services Institute, London, May 31, 2013,
https://rusi.org/commentary/why-woolwich-matters-south-london-angle (last consulted in July 2016).

7: The Ambiguous Role of Frustration in Radicalization

1. See Khosrokhavar (1997). That statement was true a decade and a half ago
and remains so. Apart from a small minority of Salafists inculcated with the Wah-
habite version of Islam, the great majority of young people know almost nothing
about the religion of Allah and its past.

8: The European Model of Radicalization

1. That is how the intelligence services sometimes designate adherence to the
fundamentalist Islam of the Salafists, who reject secular society without embracing violent action.

2. "Exclusif—Transcription des conversations entre Mohamed Merah et les
négociateurs," *Libération*, July 17, 2012, www.liberation.fr/societe/2012/07/17
/transcription-des-conversations-entre-mohamed-merah-et-les-negociateurs
_833784 (last consulted in July 2016). Adrien Oster, "Un livre et une enquête dif-
fusée sur M6 révèlent les question soulevées par Abdelghani Merah, frère de
Mohamed," *Le Huffington Post*, Nov. 10, 2012, www.huffingtonpost.fr/2012/11/09

/mohamed-abdelghani-abdelkader-souad-merah-frere-terroriste-enquete
-exclusive_n_2098875.html (last consulted in July 2016).

3. "Nouvelles révélations: Merah n'était pas un 'loup solitaire,'" *La Dépêche.fr*, Aug. 23, 2012, www.ladepeche.fr/article/2012/08/23/1424173-nouvelles-revelations-merah-n-etait-pas-un-loup-solitaire.html (last consulted in May 2014).

4. On the whole, girls have a different kind of life. Granted, small minorities of female delinquents break away and attempt to imitate the male model, if only to become economically autonomous from their families and achieve a middle-class level of consumption. But in most cases, the greater supervision to which girls are subject protects them from deviant behavior, and because they are more serious in their studies than their brothers, they are also able to find employment.

5. A list of them and a description of their ideas can be found in Khosrokhavar (2009, 2011).

6. See the case of Adlène Hicheur, who is closest to that model. Bastien Za-ouche, "Hicheur s'est fourvoyé dans l'islam radical," *L'Express*, Mar. 31, 2012, www .lexpress.fr/actualite/societe/justice/hicheur-s-est-fourvoye-dans-l-islam-radical _1099876.html (last consulted in July 2016). In the interview I had with him in prison in 2012, that sense of unreality seemed to persist.

7. Eric Albert, "Soldat décapité à Londres: Deux hommes reconnus coupables," *Le Monde* with Agence France Presse, Dec. 19, 2013, www.lemonde.fr /europe/article/2013/12/19/soldat-decapite-a-londres-deux-hommes-reconnus -coupables_4337489_3214.html (last consulted in July 2016).

8. "Royaume-Uni: Le meurtrier du soldat Rigby raconte son 'adoration d'al-Qaida,'" *Le Monde*, Dec. 9, 2013, www.lemonde.fr/europe/article/2013/12/09/roy aume-uni-le-meurtrier-du-soldat-rigby-raconte-son-adoration-d-al-qaida_3528174 _3214.html (last consulted in July 2016).

9. Jonathan Githens-Mazer, "Why Woolwich Matters: The South London Angle," *RUSI Analysis*, Royal United Services Institute, London, May 31, 2013, https://rusi.org/commentary/why-woolwich-matters-south-london-angle (last consulted in July 2016).

10. Christophe Cornevin, "Comment les djihadistes français sont recrutés sur Internet," *Le Figaro*, Jan. 24, 2014; Sam Jones, "Jihad by Social Media," *Financial Times Magazine*, Mar. 28, 2014.

11. A Tunisian was deported following a procedure of utmost urgency by the Ministry of the Interior, for having attempted to recruit candidates to jihad among French young people in Grenoble. See "Expulsion d'un Tunisien qui recruitait des djihadistes à Grenoble," *Le Monde* with Agence France Presse, June 14, 2014, www .lemonde.fr/societe/article/2014/06/14/expulsion-d-un-tunisien-qui-recrutait-des -djihadistes-a-grenoble_4438325_3224.html (last consulted in July 2016).

12. Haroon Siddique, "Jihadi Recruitment Video for Islamist Terror Group Isis Features Three Britons," *The Guardian*, June 20, 2014.

13. Dounia Bouzar (2014) places particular emphasis on the question of identity, at the expense of the self-assertive dimension, in plans for destruction.

14. Magali Judith, "Djihad en Syrie: 'Nos enfants sont des adolescents manipulés, sous le joug de prédateurs terroristes,'" *Le Monde*, May 2, 2014, www.lemonde

.fr/societe/article/2014/05/02/djihad-en-syrie-nos-enfants-sont-des-adolescents -manipules-sous-le-joug-de-predateurs-terroristes_4410915_3224.html (last consulted in July 2016).

15. For Salafists, modern democracy is a form of idolatry, because the legal and the political should be under God's authority, and His commandments on that subject are set down in the Quran and the Hadith.

16. The literature on radical Islamists generally affirms the "normality" of the overwhelming majority. The problem is that this literature is based on studies of jihadism in the early 2000s, when the al-Qaeda model dominated; it overlooks the new paradigm that has appeared since then, in which jihadists are more dispersed and often more fragile psychologically. See, for example, Diego Gambetta (2005) and Marc Sageman (2004, 2008), whose works bear the stamp of the classic type of jihadism.

17. In the prisons near big cities, especially in Île-de-France and near Lyon and Marseille, the proportion of prisoners who embrace the religion of Allah (whether they are observant or not) fluctuates between 40 and 70 percent of the prison population. There are no statistics to corroborate that estimate, which is based on indirect indications (the opinion of imams, meals served during the Ramadan fast, Arabic family and given names, and the assessments of guards in direct contact with prisoners; see Khosrokhavar 2004).

9: The New Radicalism on the March

1. Aaron Y. Zelin, "ICSR Insight: European Foreign Fighters in Syria," International Centre for the Study of Radicalism and Political Violence, Department of War Studies, Kings College, London, Apr. 2, 2013, http://icsr.info/2013/04/icsr -insight-european-foreign-fighters-in-syria-2 (last consulted in July 2016). This study estimates the number of European jihadists in Syria at between 135 and 590 individuals, 30 to 92 of them French. Since then, the numbers have grown considerably. According to new sources, some 1,500 to 2,000 Europeans have enlisted in Syria, including several hundred French. See "Syrie: De plus en plus d'Européens grossissent les rangs djihadistes," *Le Point*, Dec. 5, 2013, www.lepoint.fr/monde /syrie-de-plus-en-plus-d-europeens-grossissent-les-rangs-djihadistes-05-12-2013 -1765276_24.php (last consulted in July 2016).

2. According to some estimates, there are several hundred Libyan jihadists, more than a thousand Tunisians, several hundred Egyptians, a thousand Saudis, a few dozen Algerians, and several dozen Moroccans. The countries that were the theater for the Arab Spring in 2010–2011 have a much larger number of followers of jihad in Syria, particularly as a result of the failure of the central state. See "The Phenomenon of Foreign Fighters from the Arab World in the Syrian Civil War," The Meir Amit Intelligence and Terrorism Information Center at the Israeli Intelligence and Heritage Commemoration Center, May 2014, www.terrorism-info .org.il/en/article/20646 (consulted in July 2016).

3. José Garçon and Jean-Pierre Perrin, "Les Américains n'ont pas fabriqué ben Laden," *Libération*, Sept. 27, 2004; Fishman 2008.

4. "'La France a une responsabilité historique' en Syrie," *Le Monde*, July 27, 2013.

5. "From Soccer to Jihad: German Football Talent Killed in Syria," *Spiegel Online International*, Nov. 18, 2013, www.spiegel.de/international/germany/former -german-soccer-player-killed-in-syrian-civil-war-a-934148.html (consulted in July 2016).

6. See "Concern over Islamist Letters Sent to Muslim Inmates," *Copenhagen Post*, Oct. 4, 2013, http://cphpost.dk/news/concern-over-islamist-letters-sent-to -muslim-inmates.7182.html (last consulted in July 2016).

10: Radicalization Versus Deradicalization

1. "Le plan de lutte contre le djihad entre en action," *Le Nouvel Observateur* with Agence France Presse, Apr. 30, 2014.

Conclusion

1. It began earlier in France, in 1995, with eight attacks between July and October, which killed eight and injured some two hundred.

BIBLIOGRAPHY

Adraoui, Mohamed-Ali. 2013. *Du Golfe aux banlieues: Le salafisme mondialisé.* Paris: Presses Universitaires de France.

André-Dessornes, Carole. 2013. *Les femmes-martyres dans le monde arabe: Liban, Palestine et Irak.* Paris: L'Harmattan.

Baker, Abdul Haqq. 2011. *Extremists in Our Midst: Confronting Terror.* Basingstoke, UK: Palgrave Macmillan.

Bakker, Edwin, Christophe Paulussen, and Eva Entenmann. 2013. "Dealing with European Foreign Fighters in Syria: Governance Challenges and Legal Implications." The Hague: International Centre for Counter-Terrorism, Research Paper, December 16.

Bergen, Peter. 2006. *The Osama bin Laden I Know: An Oral History of al-Qaeda's Leader.* New York: Free Press.

Borum, Randy. 2011. "Radicalization into Violent Extremism," part 1, "A Review of Social Science Theories." *Journal of Strategic Security* 4, no. 4: 7–36.

Bouzar, Dounia. 2014. *Désamorcer l'islam radical: Ces dérives sectaires qui défigurent l'islam.* Ivry-sur-Seine: Éditions de l'Atelier.

Bronner, Gérald. 2009. *La pensée extrême: Comment des hommes ordinaires deviennent des fanatiques.* Paris: Denoël.

Cannac, René. 1961. *Aux sources de la révolution russe: Netchaïev, du nihilisme au terrorisme,* preface by André Mazon. Paris: Payot.

Cook, David, ed. 2010. *Jihad and Martyrdom.* London: Routledge.

Coolsaet, Rik. 2005. "Radicalisation and Europe's Counter-Terrorism Strategy." Address given at the Transatlantic Dialogue on Terrorism, Center for Strategic and International Studies, Washington, DC, and Clingendael (Netherlands Institute of International Relations), The Hague, Dec. 8–9.

Crenshaw, Martha. 2005. "Political Explanations." In *Addressing the Causes of Terrorism,* vol. 1 of Club de Madrid Series on Democracy and Terrorism, pp. 13–19. Madrid: Club de Madrid.

Dartnell, Michael. 1995. *Action Directe: Ultra-Left Terrorism in France, 1979–1987.* London: Cass.

Devereux, Georges. 1970. *Essais d'ethnopsychiatrie générale.* Paris: Gallimard.

Dubet, François. 2008 (1987). *La galère, jeunes en survie.* Paris: Seuil.

European Commission. 2014. *Preventing Radicalisation to Terrorism and Violent Extremism: Strengthening the EU's Response*. Brussels: European Commission, COM (2013), 941 final.

Filiu, Jean-Pierre. 2006. *Les frontières du Jihad*. Paris: Fayard.

Fishman, Brian, ed. 2008. *Bombers, Bank Accounts, and Bleedout: al-Qa'ida's Routes in and out of Iraq*. West Point, NY: Harmony Project, Combating Terrorism Center at West Point.

Gambetta, Diego, ed. 2005. *Making Sense of Suicide Missions*. Oxford: Oxford University Press.

Juergensmeyer, Mark. 2003. *Terror in the Mind of God: The Global Rise of Religious Violence*. Berkeley: University of California Press.

Kepel, Gilles. 2003. *Jihad: Expansion et déclin de l'islamisme*. Paris: Gallimard.

Khosrokhavar, Farhad. 1997. *L'islam des jeunes*. Paris: Flammarion.

———. 2004. *L'islam dans les prisons*. Paris: Balland.

———. 2009. *Inside Jihadism: Understanding Jihadi Movements Worldwide*. Boulder, CO: Paradigm.

———. 2011. *Jihadist Ideology: The Anthropological Perspective*. Aarhus, Denmark: Centre for Studies in Islamism and Radicalisation, Department of Political Science, Aarhus University.

———. 2013. "Radicalization in Prison: The French Case." *Politics, Religion & Ideology* 14, no. 3:284–306, http://dx.doi.org/10.1080/21567689.2013.792654 (consulted on July 2, 2016).

Lapeyronnie, Didier. 2008. *Le ghetto urbain: Ségrégation, violence, pauvreté en France aujourd'hui*. Paris: Robert Laffont.

Laske, Karl. 2012. *La mémoire du plomb*. Paris: Stock.

Leiken, Robert S., and Steven Brooke. 2006. "The Quantitative Analysis of Terrorism and Immigration: An Initial Exploration." *Terrorism and Political Violence* 18: 503–21.

McCauley, Clark, and Sophia Moskalenko. 2008. "Mechanisms of Political Radicalization: Pathways Towards Terrorism." *Terrorism and Political Violence* 20, no. 3: 415–33.

———. 2011. *Friction: How Radicalization Happens to Them and Us*. Oxford: Oxford University Press.

Merah, Abdelghani, with Mohamed Sifaoui. 2012. *Mon frère ce terroriste*. Paris: Calmann-Lévy.

O'Neill, Sean, and Daniel McGrory. 2006. *The Suicide Factory: Abu Hamza and the Finsbury Park Mosque*. London: Harper Perennial.

Pape, Robert. 2006. *Dying to Win: The Strategic Logic of Suicide Terrorism*. New York: Random House.

Patricot, Aymeric. 2013. *Les Petits Blancs: Un voyage dans la France d'en bas*. Paris: Plein Jour.

Pavey, Eleanor. 2006. "Les kamikazes sri lankais." *Cultures & Conflits* 63 (Fall): 135–54.

Pedahzur, Ami. 2004. "Toward an Analytical Model of Suicide Terrorism: A Comment." *Terrorism and Political Violence* 16, no. 4: 814–44.

Rivoire, Jean-Baptiste. 2011. *Le Crime de Tibhirine, révélations sur les responsables.* Paris: La Découverte.

Rougier, Bernard. 2004. *Le jihad au quotidien.* Paris: Presses Universitaires de France.

Sageman, Marc. 2004. *Understanding Terror Networks.* Philadelphia: University of Pennsylvania Press.

———. 2008. *Leaderless Jihad: Terror Networks in the Twenty-First Century.* Philadelphia: University of Pennsylvania Press.

Salafi, Abu Ameenah Abdur Rahman as-, and Abdul Haq al-Ashanti. 2011. *Abdullah El-Faisal al-Jamaiki: A Critical Study of His Statements, Errors and Extremism in Takfeer.* Luton: Jamiah Media.

Savoie, Pierre. 2011. *RG: La traque d'Action directe.* Paris: Nouveau Monde éditions.

Silber, Mitchel D., and Arvin Bhatt. 2007. *Radicalization in the West: The Homegrown Threat.* New York City Police Department, Intelligence Division.

Steiner, Anne, and Loïc Debray. 2006. *RAF: Guérilla urbaine en Europe occidentale.* Paris: Éditions l'Échappée.

Thomson, David. 2014. *Les Français jihadistes.* Paris: Les Arènes.

Vareilles, Thierry. 2005. *Histoire d'attentats politiques, de l'an 44 av. Jésus-Christ à nos jours.* Paris: L'Harmattan.

Wieviorka, Michel. 1988. *Sociétés et terrorisme.* Paris: Fayard.

Wilner, Alex S., and Claire-Jehanne Dubouloz. 2010. "Homegrown Terrorism and Transformative Learning: An Interdisciplinary Approach to Understanding Radicalization." *Global Change, Peace & Security* 22, no. 1: 33–51.

Zarate, Juan C. 2013. *Treasury's War: The Unleashing of a New Era of Financial Warfare.* New York: PublicAffairs.

INDEX

ABOUT THE AUTHOR

Farhad Khosrokhavar is the director of studies at the School for Advanced Studies in the Social Sciences in Paris. An expert on contemporary Iran and Islam in France, he lives in Paris.

ABOUT THE TRANSLATOR

Jane Marie Todd is an award-winning translator of more than seventy books. She lives in Portland, Oregon.

PUBLISHING IN
THE PUBLIC INTEREST

Thank you for reading this book published by The New Press. The New Press is a nonprofit, public interest publisher. New Press books and authors play a crucial role in sparking conversations about the key political and social issues of our day.

We hope you enjoyed this book and that you will stay in touch with The New Press. Here are a few ways to stay up to date with our books, events, and the issues we cover:

- Sign up at www.thenewpress.com/subscribe to receive updates on New Press authors and issues and to be notified about local events
- Like us on Facebook: www.facebook.com /newpressbooks
- Follow us on Twitter: www.twitter.com/thenewpress

Please consider buying New Press books for yourself; for friends and family; or to donate to schools, libraries, community centers, prison libraries, and other organizations involved with the issues our authors write about.

The New Press is a 501(c)(3) nonprofit organization. You can also support our work with a tax-deductible gift by visiting www.thenewpress.com/donate.